D1557374

THE PRACTICE OF CLINICAL HEALTH PSYCHOLOGY

PSYCHOLOGY PRACTITIONER GUIDEBOOKS

EDITORS

Arnold P. Goldstein, Syracuse University
Leonard Krasner, Stanford University & SUNY at Stony Brook
Sol L. Garfield, Washington University

THE PRACTICE OF CLINICAL HEALTH PSYCHOLOGY

CYNTHIA D. BELAR,
Kaiser Permanente Medical Care Program, Los Angeles

WILLIAM W. DEARDORFF,
Treatment Center for Craniomandibular Disorders, Woodland Hills

KAREN E. KELLY,
Cedars-Sinai Medical Center, Los Angeles

PERGAMON PRESS
New York · Oxford · Beijing · Frankfurt
Sao Paulo · Sydney · Tokyo · Toronto

U.S.A.	Pergamon Press, Maxwell House, Fairview Park, Elmsford, New York 10523, U.S.A.
U.K.	Pergamon Press, Headington Hill Hall, Oxford OX3 0BW, England
PEOPLE'S REPUBLIC OF CHINA	Pergamon Press, Room 4037, Qianmen Hotel, Beijing, People's Republic of China
FEDERAL REPUBLIC OF GERMANY	Pergamon Press, Hammerweg 6, D-6242 Kronberg, Federal Republic of Germany
BRAZIL	Pergamon Editora, Rua Eça de Queiros, 346, CEP 04011, Paraiso, São Paulo, Brazil
AUSTRALIA	Pergamon Press Australia, P.O. Box 544, Potts Point, N.S.W. 2011, Australia
JAPAN	Pergamon Press, 8th Floor, Matsuoka Central Building, 1-7-1 Nishishinjuku, Shinjuku-ku, Tokyo 160, Japan
CANADA	Pergamon Press Canada, Suite No. 271, 253 College Street, Toronto, Ontario, Canada M5T 1R5

Copyright © 1987 Pergamon Books Inc.

All Rights Reserved. No part of this publication may be reproduced, stored in a retrieval system or transmitted in any form or by any means: electronic, electrostatic, magnetic tape, mechanical, photocopying, recording or otherwise, without permission in writing from the publishers.

First printing 1987

Library of Congress Cataloging in Publication Data
Belar, Cynthia D.
The practice of clinical health psychology.
(Psychology practitioner guidebooks)
Bibliography: p.
Includes index.
1. Clinical health psychology.   2. Clinical
health psychology—Practice.   I. Deardorff,
William W.   II. Kelly, Karen E.   III. Title.
IV. Series. [DNLM: 1. Psychology, Clinical.
WM 105 B426p]
R726.7.B45   1987   610'.19   86-30500
ISBN 0-08-034678-2
ISBN 0-08-034677-4 (soft)

*Printed and bound in Great Britain by
Hazell Watson & Viney Limited,
Member of the BPCC Group,
Aylesbury, Bucks*

To my parents, Herbert and Glennie Belar, the wisest people I know.
To my husband, Jean-Louis Monfraix, for his loving patience.

C. D. B.

To my parents, for their love and encouragement. To Saul Spiro, Harold Dengerink, and Herbert Cross, for providing me with a firm scientific and clinical grounding in health psychology. To Cynthia Belar, for further shaping these skills.

W. W. D.

To my parents, for their continued love and support.
To my good friends Mark, Marge, Lisbeth, Joyce, and Kathleen, for always being there.

K. E. K.

Contents

Preface   xi

Acknowledgements   xiii

1. DEFINING THE FIELD OF CLINICAL HEALTH
   PSYCHOLOGY   1
   Historical Perspectives in Clinical Health Psychology   3
   The Growth of Health Psychology   4
   Psychology's Role in Health Care   5
   Current Roles and Functions of Clinical Health Psychologists   7
   Suggested Readings   10

2. PREPARING TO BECOME A CLINICAL HEALTH
   PSYCHOLOGIST: ACQUIRING SPECIFIC CONTENT   11
   Health Psychology Training Programs   11
   Acquiring Background Information and Training   13
   Suggested Readings   17

3. BECOMING A CLINICAL HEALTH PSYCHOLOGIST:
   PERSONAL AND PROFESSIONAL ISSUES   18
   Formalized Aspects of Health Care Settings   19
   Informal Aspects of Health Care Settings   22
   Special Issues in Professional Behavior   23
   Personal Characteristics   26
   Suggested Readings   30

4. ETHICAL ISSUES IN THE PRACTICE OF CLINICAL
   HEALTH PSYCHOLOGY   31
   Principle 1. Responsibility   31
   Principle 2. Competence   34
   Principle 3. Moral and Legal Standards   37
   Principle 4. Public Statements   38

Principle 5. Confidentiality   40
Principle 6. Welfare of the Consumer   41
Principle 7. Professional Relationships   46
Principle 8. Assessment Techniques   47
Suggested Readings   50

5.   MALPRACTICE RISKS IN CLINICAL HEALTH
     PSYCHOLOGY   52
     Psychological Malpractice   53
     Areas of Malpractice Risk in Clinical Health Psychology   55
     Summary and Conclusions   68
     Suggested Readings   68

6.   CLINICAL HEALTH PSYCHOLOGY ASSESSMENT   69
     A Model for Assessment in Clinical Health Psychology   71
     Targets of Assessment   72
     Integrating Basic Assessment Information   78
     Methods of Assessment   81
     Achieving the Goals of Assessment: Understanding the
        Patient   87
     Suggested Readings   88

7.   INTERVENTION STRATEGIES IN CLINICAL HEALTH
     PSYCHOLOGY   89
     Patient Targets   89
     Environmental Targets   90
     Choosing Targets for Intervention   93
     Intervention Strategies   95
     Suggested Readings   109

8.   SPECIAL ISSUES IN ASSESSMENT AND INTERVENTION   111
     Clarifying the Referral Question   111
     Dealing with Poorly Timed Referral Requests   115
     Dumping and Turfing   116
     Problems in Obtaining Background Information   116
     Initial Contact with the Patient   119
     Boundary Issues in Clinical Health Psychology   125
     Special Issues in Assessment   126
     Special Considerations in Treatment   129
     Issues of Disposition   130

9. FUTURE ISSUES FOR CLINICAL HEALTH PSYCHOLOGY   135
      Technological Advances   135
      Development of the Profession   136
      Changes in Psychiatry   138
      Changes in the Health Care System   138
      Suggested Readings   139

    References   140

    Appendix A: Journals Relevant to Clinical Health Psychology   149

    Appendix B: Medical Abbreviations   151

    Appendix C: Professional and Disease-Specific Organizations 155

    Author Index   159

    Subject Index   163

    About the Authors   166

    Psychology Practitioner Guidebooks List   167

Preface

The field of health psychology has mushroomed during the past decade, with a concomitant increase in the number of new publications. These include refereed scholarly journals (e.g., *Journal of Behavioral Medicine, Journal of Health Psychology*) and a number of texts that provide either analyses of the conceptual and empirical bases of the field or disease-oriented reviews of the literature (e.g., Feuerstein, Labbé & Kuczmierczyk, 1986; Gentry, 1984; Millon, Green, & Meagher, 1982a; Prokop & Bradley, 1981; Stone, Cohen, & Adler, 1979). Recently there have appeared more practically oriented materials for professionals wishing to develop expertise in specific clinical problems in health psychology (e.g., Blanchard and Andrasik's excellent 1985 guidebook on headache, and Holzman and Turk's comprehensive 1986 handbook on pain management). However, there has been a dearth of general-practice guides in the area, a gap the present work attempts to fill.

The focus of this book has been limited to clinical health psychology practice issues related to treatment in outpatient and inpatient settings. The issues dealt with (e.g., core content, professional roles, ethics, malpractice, assessment, and intervention) represent those areas we have found to be of special importance in clinical practice. Throughout the book we have attempted to identify common pitfalls in practice and to provide ideas on how to effectively manage these areas. It was beyond the scope and purpose of this book to include other areas of clinical health psychology practice such as applications to industry, political involvement, program consultation, and prevention programs even though many psychologists are involved in a number of these different types of practice.

This guidebook is not designed for the novice clinician but is intended for the clinical student or practicing professional psychologist who wishes to develop special expertise in clinical health psychology. It might also be useful to other mental health professionals who want to retool for practice with medical–surgical populations and environments. It is best viewed as an overview of the field, and it is written with an underlying assumption of competence in basic clinical skills on the part of the reader. We have attempted to delineate specific issues and potential problems in the practice of clinical health psychology, with suggestions offered where appropriate. Each case example described is one with which one of us has had personal experience. Reference materials are given for further study in each of the major areas.

The second and third authors of this volume contributed equally to its preparation, and are thus listed in alphabetical order.

Acknowledgements

Special acknowledgements are given to W. Doyle Gentry for stimulating my interest as an intern in what we then termed *medical psychology*; to Joe Matarazzo for his sustaining influence on the field and on my own thinking; to Nathan Perry for supporting my professional growth and my development of training programs in clinical health psychology at the University of Florida; to Philip Shulman for his encouragement of continued development of services and training at Kaiser Permanente; and to all my students whose intellectual curiosity, need for guidance, and enthusiasm for learning have enhanced my learning and commitment to the field.

C. D. B.

Special acknowledgements are given to B. Kent Houston, my mentor and friend, for making major contributions to my education and professional development; to David S. Holmes for furthering my critical thinking and interest in writing; and to Cynthia Belar for her unyielding knowledge and sound clinical judgments, which have added depth to my professional skills.

K. E. K.

Chapter 1
Defining the Field of Clinical Health Psychology

Any new area of professional practice must wrestle with defining the scope and nature of its body of knowledge and the application thereof to clinical service. Clinical health psychology is no exception. During its development as a distinct field of practice, there has been a history of searching for an adequate label that practitioners can embrace. Millon (1982) was the first to offer a concise definition of *clinical health psychology* that captured the elements of the science and its applications:

> The application of knowledge and methods from all substantive fields of psychology to the promotion and maintenance of mental and physical health of the individual and to the prevention, assessment, and treatment of all forms of mental and physical disorder in which psychological influences either contribute to or can be used to relieve an individual's distress or dysfunction. (p. 9)

This definition represents a merging of clinical psychology, with its focus on the assessment and treatment of individuals in distress, and the content field of *health psychology*, which is defined as

> . . . the aggregate of the specific educational, scientific, and professional contributions of the discipline of psychology to the promotion and maintenance of health, the prevention and treatment of illness, and the identification of etiologic and diagnostic correlates of health, illness and related dysfunctions. (Matarazzo, 1980, p. 815)

Although professional activity in clinical health psychology has long preceded the usage of this term, we believe this designation best describes this area of practice for psychologists. As Millon (1982) stated, "The label chosen to represent the field is of no minor import; it will certainly shape its focus as a research realm and its viability and character as a service profession" (p. 9). Related labels are either inappropriate, confusing, or too narrow. Examples of these terms include *behavioral medicine, medical psychology,* and *psychosomatic medicine.*

Behavioral medicine is an interdisciplinary field. A psychologist cannot practice medicine; as psychologists, we can only practice psychology. This is evident from the most commonly accepted definition of behavioral medicine, which is

> the interdisciplinary field concerned with the development and integration of behavioral and biomedical science, knowledge and technique relevant to health and illness and the application of this knowledge and these techniques to prevention, diagnosis, treatment and rehabilitation. (Schwartz & Weiss, 1978, p. 250)

Stemming from a landmark conference at Yale University in February 1977, and further refined at a meeting of the National Academy of Sciences in April 1978, this definition was specifically intended by the leaders in the field to *not* represent either a single theoretical orientation (behavioral) or a single discipline (medicine). However, it is frequently interpreted as one or both of these by the less well informed (and sometimes asserted as such by the more chauvinistic). Nevertheless, all health psychologists and all clinical health psychologists are contributors to the field of behavioral medicine, as are social workers, nurses, epidemiologists, physicians, and all members of other disciplines who choose to practice, to teach, to develop policy, or to conduct research related to the integration of behavioral and biomedical sciences relevant to health and illness.

Another term, *medical psychology,* can be confusing in that it has at least three well-accepted meanings and conveys narrowness of focus (e.g., excluding psychologists practicing primarily with dental populations):

1. "the practice of psychology in the medical school establishment" (Gentry & Matarazzo, 1981, p. 12)
2. "the study of psychological factors related to any and all aspects of physical health, illness and its treatment at the individual, groups and systems level" (Asken, 1979, p. 67)
3. traditional psychiatry in Great Britain

The term *psychosomatic medicine* has historically been the most prominent. Originally intended to refer to the unity of mind–body relationships, it usually conveys the notion of psychological causation of physiological disorders to most health professionals and to the public, carrying with it some pejorative overtones. Again, use of the term *medicine* would be inappropriate for the practitioner of the discipline of psychology.

Other labels found in the field such as *pediatric psychology, rehabilitation psychology,* and *neuropsychology* are pertinent to very narrow content and practice areas and, of course, do not convey the broad range of application in this area.

In summary, we believe that the term *clinical health psychology* best conveys the breadth of the field (health) while designating a focus on applied practice with individuals in distress (clinical). The practice is discipline-specific (psychology); however, the recognition that the field of health includes many other disciplines makes much of the following information also relevant to those practitioners.

HISTORICAL PERSPECTIVES IN CLINICAL HEALTH PSYCHOLOGY

In Western culture, the roots of clinical health psychology date back to the fifth century BC and the Hippocratic school of medicine. Health was viewed as a natural balance of physical and emotional aspects, mediated by a harmonious mixture of the humors (phlegm, choler, blood, melancholy). It was in 1747 that Gaub, a professor of medicine, wrote "the reason why a sound body becomes ill, or an ailing body recovers, very often lies in the mind" (cited in Lipowski, 1977, p. 234). During the years between 1920 and 1950, the more formalized field of psychosomatic medicine emerged. Two major frameworks dominated: psychodynamic and psychophysiologic. One of the best representatives of the psychodynamic viewpoint was Franz Alexander (1950), who, inspired by psychoanalytic theory, developed a specificity theory of illness. Specific unresolved unconscious conflicts were thought to produce specific somatic disorders in this *nuclear conflict theory* (e.g., frustrated oral and dependency needs result in duodenal ulcer). In the area of psychophysiology, Harold G. Wolff (1953) utilized highly innovative experimental designs to study the effects of psychological stimuli on physiological processes, developing a theory of psychological stress that he applied to a wide range of somatic diseases. For example, he noted that during subjects' discussion of relationship problems (stress), resentment was associated with increased blood pressure, whereas despair or depression were associated with lowered blood pressure (Wolff & Wolf, 1951). These results were particularly true of hypertensives. In general, this era was marked by the passage of mind–body processes from the province of philosophy and religion, to become respectable subjects of scientific inquiry.

The past three decades have been marked by a decrease in the influence of psychodynamic theories, an increased focus on psychophysiological processes, the addition of social and ecological dimensions, and the development of psychological interventions to prevent or ameliorate disease and improve the health care system. Psychology as a discipline has made significant contributions to this endeavor.

From the experimental psychology laboratory, we have obtained information about learning and bodily processes, with subsequent successful efforts at physiological self-regulation via biofeedback. Studies of cognitive processes have revealed the importance of meaning, belief systems, information processing, and attention to health issues such as compliance, help seeking, and pain tolerance. Research on psychoendocrinology has helped us to understand relationships between physiological processes and emotions, and behavior change technology has been applied in attempts to reduce behavioral health risks. Some of the most exciting developments are now occurring in the rapidly developing field of psychoneuroimmunology, which holds the promise of delineating the mediating mechanisms between psychological processes and health (Ader, 1981).

Because a review of current psychosomatic theory and research is beyond the scope of this book, suffice it to say that the field is now characterized by an understanding of the multicausality of somatic functions and behavior, complex multivariate designs, and sophisticated psychophysiological assessments. Psychology, as the science of behavior, will continue to be an integral part of the widely accepted biopsychosocial model of health.

THE GROWTH OF HEALTH PSYCHOLOGY

As a field, health psychology mushroomed from the mid 1970s to the mid 1980s. Gentry (1984) summarized some of the possible reasons for this well-accepted fact: (a) failure of the biomedical model to adequately explain health and illness; (b) increased concern with quality of life and prevention of illness; (c) shift of focus from infectious disease to chronic disease as the major challenge in medicine, with concomitant recognition of the influence of life-style factors; (d) increased maturity of research in the behavioral sciences, including the application of learning theories to disease etiology and illness behavior; and (e) increased cost of health care and the search for alternatives to the traditional health care system.

Those of us who were involved in this rapid growth remember the fervor with which we worked to establish new professional groups. The year 1978 was a high point in this developmental process. The Academy of Behavioral Medicine was established in April, electing Neal E. Miller its first president. On November 16, 1978, we held the first organizational meeting of the Society of Behavioral Medicine in Chicago, and, at the annual meeting of the American Psychological Association (APA), we celebrated the formation of the new Division of Health Psychology. Also that year, the *Journal of Behavioral Medicine* began, under the editorship of W. Doyle Gentry.

We rejoiced at the success of our colleagues who succeeded in establishing study sections of behavioral medicine within the National Institutes of

Health for peer review of research and training grants. And we welcomed the publication of additional scientific journals (*Health Psychology*) and relevant texts for our courses (e.g., Millon, Green, & Meagher, 1982a; Prokop & Bradley, 1981; Stone, Cohen, & Adler, 1979; Weiner, 1977; Williams & Gentry, 1977).

As the field developed, our concern for quality led to the Arden House National Working Conference on Education and Training in Health Psychology, May 23–27, 1983. Chaired by Steve Weiss, this conference developed recommendations for education and training at the predoctoral, apprenticeship, and postdoctoral levels for research and professional career paths. A full report of these proceedings can be found in Stone (1983). Those of us who were instrumental in designing this conference also recognized the need for a definitive volume that would deal with the key issues raised, but in a more scholarly format. The recent work *Health Psychology: A discipline and a profession* (Stone et al., in press) attempted to do this, and the reader is referred to this source for more detailed discussions.

The 1970s and early 1980s were a time in which many of us felt we had a mission to accomplish in spreading the word about health psychology and the potential for practice in this area; however, we knew we were not the first to recognize the importance of psychological factors in health and health care.

PSYCHOLOGY'S ROLE IN HEALTH CARE

The role of the psychologist in the health care system began early in this century as that of a teacher of medical students (see Stone, 1979). The area most frequently represented was physiological psychology, as related research flourished. In general there was little special application of psychology to the problems of the health care system itself. As the field of clinical psychology developed after World War II, the focus was primarily on mental disorders. There were some studies on overutilizers of the health care system, some pathology-oriented treatment reports on classic psychosomatic disorders, and an important body of work by Janis (1958) on psychological preparation for surgery. However, it is Schofield's (1969) report on the role of psychology in the delivery of health services that marks the beginning of an explosion of this area in the psychological literature.

Until fairly recently, however, the role of clinical psychology continued to be somewhat limited. As Millon (1982) pointed out, with but few notable exceptions (e.g., Schofield, 1969), clinical psychology "was misguided in its evolution when it followed a dualistic mind–body model and thereby limited itself to ministering to the 'mentally' disordered" (1982, p.

9). In a clever reworking of Engel's well-known critique of the medical model (1977, p. 129), Millon suggested that clinical psychology's crisis stemmed from its logical inference that because behavior disorder is defined in terms of psychosocial parameters, psychologists need not be concerned with the somatic issues that lie outside psychology's responsibility and authority. This attitude divides the patient illogically and spuriously segments health care in the same manner that medicine has been criticized in the past.

Indeed, the senior author remembers well the times in the early 1970s when she was required, while attempting to establish herself in academic clinical psychology, to justify to skeptical senior professors her clinical interest in medical–surgical patients and ·the treatment of chronic pain problems. The usual question, Is this real clinical psychology?, reflected the mind–body dualism extant in the field. Actually, that process proved helpful in that it facilitated critical thinking about the field and increased sensitivity to many professional and political issues involved in extending the boundaries of professional practice.

Subsequent experiences have confirmed that mind–body dualism is as alive and well in psychology, psychiatry, and psychiatric social work as it is in general medicine. Remarkable numbers of mental-health practitioners feel no need to review a patient's medical chart prior to undertaking psychotherapy. Many such clinicians actually dislike dealing with medical–surgical patients because these patients have "real" (meaning insoluble?) problems. When consultations are conducted by these practitioners, findings are often expressed in either–or and functional versus organic terminology. Most disheartening is when administrative personnel, who are responsible for health policy formation and implementation, convey the belief that a health care system's psychological services unit should *not* be responsible for psychological services related to other (nonpsychiatric) medical–surgical units. In reference to neuropsychological assessment or psychophysiological approaches to headache, we have heard statements asserting, "The neurologists should be responsible for those services." In our experience, this tends to occur in systems where psychiatrists are in control of psychological services and where the particular psychiatrists involved have strong desires to keep psychology in a subordinate role.

Mind–body dualism is also deeply ingrained in health policies. There is usually a division in coverage between *mental health* and *medical–surgical health* insurance benefits, with mental health coverage usually less extensive. Conceptually, this poses difficult problems when attempting to determine which coverage is responsible for such things as management of a hypertensive medication compliance problem, biofeedback treatment of surgically induced fecal incontinence, or cognitive–behavioral management of headache. Typically, these services are covered only under mental health benefits, a health policy that tends to perpetuate rigid mind–body dualism. For example, within the Southern California Kaiser Permanente system, a region of the nation's largest health maintenance organization and nongovernmental health care system, it is quite clear that *all psychological counseling* is covered under the *mental health benefit* suggesting that such treatments are only appropriate for mental health problems.

Dualism is also found in administrative structures, as evidenced by geographically separate clinics. Many mental health clinics are actually located at some distance from the medical center, and thus from the mainstream of health care.

Given the tenor of the times, it should be of no surprise that, in the early years of health psychology, many clinical psychologists were searching for a professional group that provided mutually shared concerns and goals, as well as opportunities to cross-fertilize that were not available under more traditional structures. (As Morrow and Clayman, 1982, found in their survey of Division of Health Psychology members, almost half of the nearly 1,500 respondents were clinical psychologists by training.)

Clearly, the attitudinal set of mind–body dualism and related administrative issues have significant implications for the professional functioning and practice of clinical health psychologists, some of which will be addressed in a later chapter. As we begin to deal with various issues of training, professional status, and practice, the reader is advised to be alert to the instances in which mind–body dualism seeps into our own writing—a product of our language system, our cultural heritage, and our own struggle to integrate psychological and physiological concepts.

Our model of clinical health psychology thus actually incorporates mental health psychology as a complete subset in the domain of clinical health psychology. However, for the purposes of this book, we have chosen to deal primarily with practice in medical–surgical settings. In general, we shall assume existing expertise in more traditional areas of professional, clinical, or counseling psychology.

CURRENT ROLES AND FUNCTIONS OF CLINICAL HEALTH PSYCHOLOGISTS

Although there are no survey data specifically on clinical health psychologists, we do have information about activities of health psychologists from two sources: the work of Morrow and Clayman (1982) in their survey of Division of Health Psychology members (1,477 respondents) and the Stabler and Mesibov (1984) survey of both Division of Health Psychology and Division 12, Section 5 (Pediatric Psychologists) memberships (686 respondents). One half to two thirds of psychologists in the three samples obtained their original training in clinical psychology (social experimental, and developmental psychology were the next most frequently mentioned training backgrounds). Although the data are not broken down by training background, it appears clear that the most common work settings were universities, medical centers, and private practice, and these accounted for approximately 60% of all respondents. In all groups, the most frequent activity appeared to be therapy, accounting for approximately 25% to 35% of professional time. For the health psychologists in both samples, research was the next most frequent function (15% to 25% of time). For the pediatric psychology sample, the most frequent activity was functioning as a diagnostician (20% to 25% of time; health psychologists spent only about 10% of time in diagnostics). Activities such as teaching (around 15%), consulting (around 15%), and administration (5% to 10% were also represented.

Obviously, clinical health psychologists engage in the same broad range of functions as more traditional clinical psychologists, with a significant portion of their time being spent in diagnostic and therapeutic activities. However, these data do not reflect the heterogeneity of the roles and functions involved. These can best be illustrated by giving examples of employment positions which already exist.

Dr. S. J. developed and directs an inpatient unit for children with diabetes at an academic medical center. She designs clinical interventions and conducts clinical research related to emotional, family, and behavioral aspects of diabetes and compliance to medical regimens. She trains clinical psychology predoctoral students, interns, postdoctoral fellows, and residents in pediatrics and child psychiatry.

Dr. J. R. directs the psychological services at a multidisciplinary pain clinic, providing cognitive behavioral pain classes, biofeedback training, and psychometric assessment services. He researches psychophysiologic aspects of pain, focusing on measurement and cognitive factors associated with memory for pain. He teaches neurology and anesthesiology residents.

Dr. M. J. serves as a member of a consultation–liaison team in a large health maintenance organization (HMO). In addition to providing emergency consultation services to hospital patients and staff, he is a team member in the bone marrow transplant unit and in pediatric oncology, where he consults with staff and patients on psychological issues related to patient care. In addition, he serves as coordinator for the psychiatry portion of the Family Practice Residency Program.

Dr. L. B. has a private practice and specializes in clinical neuropsychology, working with brain-injured individuals, patients with posttraumatic stress disorders, and geriatric populations.

Dr. W. M. teaches basic behavioral science to students in a college of dentistry and trains them in interviewing and in patient-management

skills. He also provides diagnostic and treatment services to a temporoman-
dibular-joint pain clinic.

Dr. M. F. conducts an industrial consulting service that offers behavioral
risk-reduction programs to large industries (e.g., work site programs for
stress, smoking, weight reduction).

Clearly, these psychologists have varied roles and functions within their
current positions. Other clinical health psychologists we have known
have engaged in the following clinical activities as part of their professional roles:

1. Assessment of candidates for penile prosthesis surgery, back surgery,
   sterilization
2. Desensitization of fears of medical and dental treatments, including
   needle phobias, fears of anesthesia, and fears of childbirth
3. Treatment to enhance coping with or control over pain, including
   chronic back pain, headache, severe burns
4. Interventions to control symptoms such as vomiting associated with
   pregnancy and chemotherapy, scratching associated with neurodermatitis, vasospasms associated with Raynaud's disease, and
   dyspnea associated with chronic obstructive pulmonary disease
5. Support groups for chronic illness, cardiac rehabilitation, and dying
   patients and their families
6. Training to overcome physical handicaps after trauma; cognitive
   retraining after stroke; training to use prosthetic devices effectively
7. Behavior-change programs for behavioral risk factors such as smoking, weight, and stress
8. Consultations and workshops to deal with issues of staff burnout,
   communication, and role conflict
9. Consultations and program development regarding patient compliance (e.g., special programs for the elderly)
10. Consultations with industry to improve behavioral health at the work
    site
11. Development of psychosocial services for oncology patients
12. Neuropsychological assessments for baseline, diagnostic, and treat-
    ment planning purposes

The range of possible clinical activities is obviously diverse. Clinical
health psychology practitioners utilize the range of diagnostic and
therapeutic techniques available to professional psychology: diagnostic
interviewing; behavioral assessments; psychometric testing; insight-
oriented psychotherapies; behavioral therapies; psychophysiological self-
regulation and biofeedback; family, marital, and group therapies; psychoeducational counseling groups; and staff-level interventions. Their
theoretical orientations include, but are not limited to, psychodynamic,
behavioral, systems, existential, and social learning theory approaches.

They deal with the problems of coping with illness; compliance; psycho-physiologic disorders; doctor–patient relationships; health care systems design; differential diagnoses; and prevention of disorders. No one clinical health psychologist is an expert in all the possible areas of practice. Nor would it be possible, within the context of this guidebook, to provide an educational background in each potential area of practice. Thus, we shall focus our comments upon more generic issues of preparation and clinical practice for the health psychologist, emphasizing process issues and pitfalls.

SUGGESTED READINGS

Engel, G. L. (1977). The need for a new medical model: A challenge for biomedicine. *Science, 196* (4286) 129–136.

Lipowski, Z. J. (1977). Psychosomatic medicine in the seventies: An overview. *American Journal of Psychiatry, 134* (3) 233–243.

Millon, T. (1982). On the nature of clinical health psychology. In T. Millon, C. J. Green, & R. B. Meagher (Eds.), *Handbook of clinical health psychology*. New York: Plenum.

Schofield, W. (1969). The role of psychology in the delivery of health services. *American Psychologist, 24*, 565–584.

Stone, G. C. (1979). Psychology and the health system. In G. C. Stone, F. Cohen, & N. Adler (Eds.), *Health Psychology*. San Francisco: Jossey-Bass.

Stone, G. C., Weiss, S. M., Matarazzo, J. D., Miller, N. E., Rodin, J., Belar, C. D., Follick, M. J., & Singer, J. E. (Eds.), (in press). *Health psychology: A discipline and a profession*. Chicago: University of Chicago Press.

Chapter 2

Preparing to Become a Clinical Health Psychologist: Acquiring Specific Content

Although clinical health psychology is not as yet defined as a specialty within the field of psychology, there is a specific body of knowledge required for research and practice within this area. The process of acquiring this information is discussed in this chapter, especially the acquisition of the necessary skills for service delivery.

HEALTH PSYCHOLOGY TRAINING PROGRAMS

Surveys of education and training in health psychology have attempted to delineate programmatic offerings at the predoctoral, internship, and postdoctoral levels. From a survey of graduate departments of psychology, Belar, Wilson, and Hughes (1982) identified 42 programs that offered predoctoral training in health psychology. Although six of these described a primary focus (e.g., a specialized degree in the area), the predominant model (almost 70%) was that of a specialized track within another area of psychology, usually clinical, counseling, or school psychology. Between 80% and 95% of the identified programs offered training in consultation, assessment, intervention, or all three areas. From a survey of APA-approved internship training programs, Gentry, Street, Masur, and Asken (1981) identified 48 programs with formal training in health psychology, although only 19 required such training. Assessment and intervention were equally emphasized. Belar and Siegel (1983) identified 43 programs offering postdoctoral training in health psychology, 90% of which emphasized applied research. A more comprehensive summary of the current state of education and training in the health psychology field and related issues can be found in Belar (in press).

Detailed program descriptions obtained from the predoctoral and postdoctoral surveys mentioned before can be found in directories of training opportunities available from the American Psychological Association (APA) (Belar & Siegel, 1984; Belar & Tavel, 1982). These reports and directories are a starting point in a search for training, but, in our opinion, much of this information is already out of date, given the growth of the field in the past few years. However, the Association of Psychology Internship Centers does publish a directory, updated yearly (Carrington, 1986), which facilitates the identification of relevant professional psychology internship programs. A number of postdoctoral programs can also be found in this directory. Other sources of information on health psychology education and training are the Education and Training Committee of the Division of Health Psychology and the Council of Health Psychology Training Directors.

Guidelines for Education and Training in Health Psychology

As indicated in chapter 1, the Arden House Conference detailed a set of recommendations for the education and training of health psychologists (Stone, 1983). Although a summary of these is beyond the scope of this guidebook, certain recommendations with respect to service provision in the field deserve highlighting.

Perhaps most importantly for the *professional practice* of health psychology (thus for clinical health psychology), the scientist–practitioner model was endorsed at every level of training. Also accepted was the model of a required 2-year postdoctoral training program for service providers in health psychology. This recommendation was based on

> (a) the rapidly developing number of interventions for specific disorders and techniques of health promotion, coupled with; (b) advances in scientific knowledge within both psychology and other relevant disciplines, and thus; (c) the magnitude of the training task required to ensure mastery. (Working Group on Postdoctoral Training for the Health Psychology Service Provider, as reported in Stone, 1983, p. 141)

In general conference delegates agreed that professional training in health psychology should include a broad set of experiences leading to knowledge and skills in the following core areas:

1. Biological bases of health systems and behavior
2. Social bases of health systems and behavior
3. Psychological bases of health systems and behavior

4. Health assessment, consultation, and intervention
5. Interdisciplinary collaboration
6. Ethical, legal, and professional issues
7. Statistics and experimental design in health research

Exposure to health care settings, a multidisciplinary faculty, and experienced professional health psychology mentors were considered crucial. Further, it was decided that programs offering such education and training should meet APA accreditation criteria. For students and practitioners interested in clinical health psychology training, a review of the conference proceedings and the APA Accreditation Handbook would be most worthwhile (APA, 1986).

Belar (1980) has described what is transportable from traditional clinical training and what needs to be added to better train graduate students to function effectively in this growing field. A basic assumption is that understanding of the fundamentals of human behavior and of the critical thinking–hypothesis testing approach to research and clinical problems can transfer to any area in which the psychologist chooses to work. The current authors support the fact that the field has adopted the scientist–practitioner model for service providers in health psychology, but we shall focus our comments on the practitioner component in keeping with the goal of a clinical guidebook. Our discussions will assume that the reader is either a fully trained professional clinician—and thus knowledgeable in such areas as diagnostics, therapy, and psychopathology—or a student in an organized professional training program.

The remainder of this chapter will cover topics of specific content relevant to clinical health psychology. In chapter 3 we shall address professional role issues and intrapersonal concerns. Specific clinical skills required in assessment and intervention will be discussed in chapters 6 and 7. However, we would like to underscore our belief that competence in research methodology is fundamental to the functioning of a clinical health psychologist. Such skills are necessary to the critical evaluation of research reports in this burgeoning area, to conduct the program evaluations so often required for accountability, and to the design of research which can make contributions to the science base of this expanding field.

ACQUIRING BACKGROUND INFORMATION AND TRAINING

Core Content Areas and Courses

With respect to specific content, one can develop one's own course of study via readings or enrollment in basic courses. The basic areas needing attention include anatomy, physiology, pathophysiology, applied pharmacology, social and psychological bases of health and disease, health policy and health care organizations, and health assessment and intervention. One needs to understand not only disease—its treatment, its course, and its emotional and behavioral correlates—but also the *context* within which the health care system operates. (Changes have been so dramatic in this area that references over 5 years old on health policy and the health care system should be considered outdated!)

Courses basic to other health professions are often useful (e.g., nursing, physical therapy, occupational therapy, respiratory therapy, health education); thus, the reader is encouraged to investigate local university or community college offerings. For the general clinical health psychologist, we have found that the courses offered in medical schools are frequently too detailed, although some might prefer the anatomy and physiology offered there. We are aware that our neuropsychologist colleagues report that the neuroanatomy courses obtained in academic medical centers have been viewed as fundamental to their areas of practice. However, in general, these courses are probably less accessible to the practicing clinician than to the graduate student.

The reader might also investigate the availability of courses in medical terminology that are frequently found in hospital administration and secretarial programs. Familiarity with the language of the health care system is a must, as is understanding the most commonly used medical abbreviations, if one is to be able to read medical charts. The senior author has witnessed scores of students and fellow professionals struggle with these language and code issues and has frequently noted the potential for negative outcomes in terms of efficiency, communication, and rapport with medical colleagues, as well as in misunderstandings of the nature of referral questions. If the clinician is planning to work in a general hospital setting, it would also be wise for her or him to obtain cardiopulmonary resuscitation (CPR) training, if she or he is not already certified in this skill. Certification and renewals are required for staff privileges. Courses are often provided by community service agencies such as the Red Cross.

It is important to remember that the goal of these didactic experiences is not to become a "junior physician." In our experience, such an attitudinal approach meets with disdain on the part of physicians, who frequently criticize their psychiatrist colleagues for not being "real physicians" when it comes to up-to-date medical knowledge and practice. Rather, an analogy might be learning enough of a foreign language to be able to get around in another country, which also means being willing and able to ask for help from the natives. We find physicians much more open to and respectful of this approach.

Reference Materials in Clinical Health Psychology

The neophyte clinical health psychologist will want to become familiar with core readings in the field. The suggested readings at the end of this chapter can provide a general background in the field. Appendix A is a list of relevant scientific journals that publish recent research and theoretical papers in health psychology. In addition, at the end of other chapters throughout this guidebook, we have provided suggested readings that detail the theoretical frameworks and empirical data related to chapter topics.

Appendix B is a list of common medical abbreviations. It is important to note, in reviewing this list, that small differences might indicate significant changes in meaning. For example, *BS* means breath sounds, whereas *bs* means bowel sounds. *Gr* indicates gravida, whereas *gr* is the abbreviation for grain. Although the context of the abbreviation can sometimes prevent errors in interpretation, note the small difference between *NC* (no change) and *N/C* (no complaints). Because different institutions have different approved medical abbreviations, it is imperative that the clinician obtain the appropriate list for his or her site of practice. For example, at the University of Florida's Shands Teaching Hospital, *AS* means aortic stenosis; at the Los Angeles Kaiser Foundation Hospital the same abbreviation means arteriosclerosis!

Worthwhile purchases include a good medical dictionary such as *Dorland's Illustrated Medical Dictionary* (1981) and an up-to-date PDR, *Physician's Desk Reference* (1986), which provides information about medication (indications, contraindications, side effects, etc.). Many clinicians find that owning a copy of the *Merck Manual* (1984) is very useful. Although this handbook is sometimes considered simplistic by the medical profession, it does provide brief descriptions of symptoms, course, laboratory findings, and prognoses of various diseases. The more expensive *Cecil Textbook of Internal Medicine* (Wyngaarden & Smith, 1985) is a classic for information on internal medicine. Taken together, these references provide a comprehensive resource list for basic study in clinical health psychology.

Additional Resources

One can also obtain information through continuing education workshops and courses. The Division of Health Psychology sponsors workshops in the field each year at the annual meeting of the APA. Likewise, the Society of Behavioral Medicine organizes workshops, as do the Biofeedback Society of America, the American Psychosomatic Society, and various other specialized groups. For example, the Arthritis Foundation has educational programs designed specifically for health professionals, in addition to those targeted to the general public. The Arthritis Health Professional Association offers yearly foundation courses in the rheumatic diseases that might be appropriate for the clinical health psychologist interested in gaining further expertise in this area.

Nearly every major disease has a related organization among whose goals is education (e.g., American Lung Association, American Cancer Society, American Tinnitus Association). Many of these groups provide substantial information at no cost. A list of names and addresses of relevant professional societies and special-interest groups can be found in Appendix C.

Finally, hospital libraries are often reservoirs of audiovisual aids provided by pharmaceutical houses. These are often used by the medical profession in obtaining continuing education credits and are at a level that psychologists can usually understand.

Supervised Training

It should be noted that didactic experiences, although necessary, are not sufficient for the practice of clinical health psychology. As is true of all professional training, the availability of appropriate role models, supervisors, and mentors is crucial. This requires a careful assessment of program faculty, or, if one is already in practice, the pursuit of an ongoing formal consultation relationship. Areas to assess in a potential supervisor are special competencies in clinical health psychology (Do they match the desired areas of practice?); sensitivity to the ethical issues of supervision; model of supervision to be employed, including goals and methods; availability to the supervisee; perspective on the field of clinical health psychology; knowledge about the health care system; and affiliation with appropriate professional groups.

The need for clinical supervision cannot be overemphasized. *First,* psychologists are bound by their ethical code to practice only in areas of competence (see chapter 4). *Second,* the wisdom acquired from clinical practice will never be totally communicable in a purely didactic framework. This would be analogous to expecting that one could learn psychotherapy via a set of readings. As all trained clinicians are aware, one of the hallmarks of professional training is a developmental process under the tutelage of "masters." *Third,* with increasing malpractice litigation, there is increased risk of a successful suit when one does not have the proper training and supervision in this area of practice (see chapter 5).

Fourth, naive or incompetent practitioners do a disservice to the rest of their profession. We have, on numerous occasions, heard stories about health care units being "spoiled" for entry by new psychologists because of previous experiences with traditionally trained (and in our view, insufficiently trained) clinical psychologists, or health psychologists who lack training in applied professional practice. Sometimes these difficulties arise from lack of specific knowledge or technique (e.g. gross misinterpretation of medical abbreviations, what physicians call "stupid questions" and "irrelevant reports," inappropriate charting, misapplication of psychodiagnostic instruments). However, they often occur because of failure to comprehend the sociopolitical features of health care. Competence in particular content areas of clinical health psychology is not sufficient, as medical settings have their own cultures that require understanding if the clinician is to be an effective participant. This culture has implications for professional role behavior. The personal conduct and attitude of the psychologist can determine the difference between the success of a service and its death due to disuse.

SUGGESTED READINGS

Feuerstein, M., Labbé, E. E., & Kuczmierczyk, A. R. (1986). *Health psychology: A psychobiological perspective.* New York: Plenum.

Gentry, W. D. (Ed.). (1984). *Handbook of behavioral medicine.* New York: Guilford Press.

Millon, T., Green, C. J., & Meagher, R. B. (Eds.). (1982). *Handbook of clinical health psychology.* New York: Plenum.

Prokop, C. K., & Bradley, L. A. (Eds.). (1981). *Medical psychology: Contributions to behavioral medicine.* New York: Academic Press.

Stone, G. C., Cohen, F., & Adler, N. E. (Eds.). (1979). *Health psychology: A handbook.* San Francisco: Jossey-Bass.

Weiner, H. (1977) *Psychobiology and human disease.* New York: American Elsevier.

Chapter 3
Becoming a Clinical Health Psychologist: Personal and Professional Issues

Knowledge of specific facts and expertise in technical clinical skills are not sufficient for the successful practice of clinical health psychology. The health care system itself, along with its various subcultures, must be understood for one to achieve credibility and acceptance as a professional health service provider. In addition, we have found that professional behaviors, attitudes, and personal characteristics of the clinician are related to performance as a clinical health psychologist. Thus, this chapter shall focus on these aspects of preparing to practice.

Clinical health psychologists frequently practice in one or more of three settings: medical–surgical hospitals, outpatient clinics, and individual private practices. Given the nature of the work, close collaboration with medical–surgical or dental specialties is required wherever the practice occurs. Historically, many psychologists have been unaware of the customs, practices, and sociopolitical issues associated with the practice of medicine or dentistry or with the hospital environment. As discussed previously, in recognition of the need for such understanding, the Arden House Conference (Stone, 1983) clearly recommended that professional training in health psychology occur in multidisciplinary health service settings, under the tutelage of experienced psychologist-mentors who themselves were bona fide members of those settings.

As an example, one requirement of a graduate-level medical psychology course taught by the senior author involved a semester-long observational experience in either an inpatient or outpatient service (e.g., dialysis unit, women's health clinic, oncology service, coronary care unit, genetic counseling clinic). The purpose of this assignment was to provide an opportunity for experiential learning about the medical setting, its language, its culture, and the nature of interdisciplinary functioning. It also provided in vivo exposure to the subjective experience of the patient, and to the stressors the health care staff experienced. Students could then compare notes with respect to such things as differences among settings, types of personnel who tended to work in them, and clinical problems likely to surface. On course evaluations, every student has reported that this experience was crucial to her or his learning. It facilitated the integration of published clinical research material, provided numerous hypotheses for future research, and stimulated ideas about potential professional roles in each of these services. Perhaps most importantly, students became much more sophisticated about the sociopolitical aspects of health care. Such observational experiences are relatively simple for students to obtain, but the practicing clinician might have to seek special arrangements with community-based practices or settings. We believe that such experiences are extremely useful.

FORMALIZED ASPECTS OF HEALTH CARE SETTINGS

To facilitate learning about the hospital setting, the APA has recently published the *Hospital Practice Primer for Psychologists* (1985a). This document provides needed information about such issues as staff privileges, organized staff membership, legal and regulatory matters, and hospital organization. Hospitals are typically organized into three systems of authority and responsibility: the board of directors (with ultimate responsibility for the activities of the hospital), the hospital administrator (responsible for the day-to-day operation of the hospital), and the medical director (responsible for all clinical care within the hospital). The hospital administrator and the medical director work together to carry out the goals of the board. Hospital professional staff report to the medical director. The board also has a number of committees, such as the credentials committee (to review credentials of professional staff), the executive committee (usually consisting of chiefs of service and department heads), the quality assurance committee (to maintain standards of practice), and the medical records committee (to insure proper documentation).

Hospital bylaws delineate qualifications for practice at the hospital, categories of professional staff, conditions of appointment, issues of quality assurance, and personnel due-process procedures. Rules and regulations for practice are detailed in accompanying documents. These usually concern documentation, standards of care, admission and discharge procedures, infection control procedures, and so forth.

In general, psychologists who wish to develop successful clinical health psychology practices should not violate these rules. For example, there are actual dress codes in some hospitals (in other settings, the code is not explicit but is just as important to understand). Identification badges could be required, and, if so, their absence is taken seriously. The senior author recalls one instance when, in a hurry to deliver a final consultation report to a ward, she left her white coat with badge behind and received an embarrassing lecture from the chief of nursing. Both the traditional white coat and identification badge are important means of quick identification of authorized personnel and are commonly used in medical settings. Another example of specific rules of the health care setting are the guidelines for making chart entries (often, in black ink only). Infractions are actually monitored by special committees. (Guidelines for charting are discussed in chapter 8). Bylaws and rules and regulations can vary across hospitals. It is imperative that the clinical health psychologist obtain copies of these documents, in order to assess what privileges and responsibilities are relevant to a particular institution.

There are various *categories of membership* of the hospital staff, as defined by hospital bylaws. Although these categories vary from institution to institution, they are generally organized as follows (APA, 1985a):

1. *Active Organized Staff.* This is the highest level of hospital privilege and responsibility. Members of this group are eligible to vote on hospital policy and may hold office. They have a full range of clinical responsibilities within their areas of competence. Often nonmedical personnel are excluded from membership within this category.
2. *Courtesy Organized Staff.* Members of this group are limited in the number of patients they may admit to the hospital and may not vote on hospital policy. Usually, these staff hold active organized status at another facility.
3. *Consulting Organized Staff.* Consulting staff members act only as *consultants* in their particular fields of expertise. They have no voting privileges and may not hold office. They may attend staff meetings and be asked to serve on various committees.
4. *Affiliate Staff.* Affiliates are generally allied health professional and ancillary or paramedical personnel. They are granted the privilege by staff to participate in patient care under direct supervision of active or courtesy staff members. They hold no voting privileges and may not serve on committees.

Although there is change nationally, psychologists are often relegated to affiliate or consulting categories (without voting or admission privileges). Psychologists have long fought for admission and discharge privileges; however, in the field of clinical health psychology, this professional issue

SIMMONS COLLEGE LIBRARIES

Interlibrary Loan for:

Ehrensworth, J.
Counseling Center.

Title:

The practice of clinical

health psychology.

Please return to the Library
Office (L101) during office
hours, M-F 8:30-4:00 pm, by
the due date:

3/25/93

Renewals may be requested.

Carol Demos
ILL Librarian
(617) 738-2242
Date: *3/2/93*

seems relatively less important—if hospitalization is required, it is usually for reasons of physical health, necessitating that the primary provider be a physician. What we find more important is the psychologist's ability to vote on rules and regulations, to participate in setting standards, to serve on staff committees, and to participate in health policy formation for the hospital.

Psychologists must apply for *staff privileges* in order to practice in a hospital. These privileges are specifically delineated in the application materials (e.g., patient admission; the writing of orders, consultation reports, and progress notes; personality and neuropsychological assessment; individual psychotherapy; group psychotherapy; hypnosis; biofeedback; emergency care; pain management; and staff development). The applicant's training, experience, and demonstrated competence are usually reviewed by the credentials committee and approved by the executive committee.

Professional behavior and practice are also governed by the standards of the Joint Commission on Accreditation of Hospitals (JCAH, 1983, 1984), by state laws that regulate practice, and by federal policy that affects health care, usually through the reimbursement process. For example, JCAH is a private nonprofit organization developed to set standards for hospitals to insure proper health care. These guidelines affect professional behavior through requirements for charting, quality assurance, staff privileges, and so forth. JCAH also requires attention to patients' rights as part of their accreditation process. (In addition to JCAH guidelines, most hospitals have a formal Patients' Bill of Rights that specifies rights to privacy, dignity, knowledge about treatment and the treating professionals, interpreter services, and so forth.) State statutes affect practice with respect to limits on confidentiality in cases of child abuse and dangerousness, as well as through licensing requirements.

Federal policy is having a profound effect on health care practices through the reimbursement system. For example, the prospective payment system (Public Law 98-21; Social Security Amendments of 1983), designed to stem the tide of increased hospital costs, calls for Medicare reimbursement to hospitals on the basis of fixed rates for diagnosis-related groups (DRGs). Although psychiatric hospitals are exempt from this reimbursement system, the settings wherein the clinical health psychologist is most likely to function are not. In addition, the new requirement that psychologists bill under Medicare Part A (hospital services, as opposed to supplementary professional fees) will result in increased interaction with hospital administrative structures. In summary, the clinician should review state statutes; JCAH guidelines; hospital bylaws, rules, and regulations; and relevant health policy prior to practice in any particular setting.

INFORMAL ASPECTS OF HEALTH CARE SETTINGS

In addition to formal structures, there are the informal rules that govern behavior in a medical setting and affect professional roles and effective functioning.

Professional Role Issues

It is important for the clinician to understand both the implicit and the explicit power hierarchy. An important question is: Who has credibility in the system? It is sad but true that some physicians who see themselves as holistic have the least credibility with their colleagues, although in some cases this may be justified. These physicians can be very anxious to collaborate and to affiliate with the beginning clinical health psychologist and can make the newcomer feel most welcomed. However, these alliances could prove disastrous if the reputation of the psychologist suffers as a result.

Stories abound of professional mistreatment of psychologists by physicians (e.g. "one down," "second class citizen," "technician"). Although the authors have a few scars in this regard, in general we have been viewed with respect as professional experts in our own areas. When dealing with more aversive situations, we have found it helpful to keep task oriented and to look for areas of mutual agreement. This usually means realizing that we all have the same goal: good patient care. Focusing interactions on this mutual goal, and not engaging in unnecessary power struggles, is not only more effective for the patient but can also be a major professional coping strategy.

Being a psychologist, and thus somewhat outside of the normal medical hierarchy, has sometimes been beneficial. As a profession, we have sufficient status to warrant attention from other health care providers but not enough to intimidate or thwart communication at various levels. It is often necessary for us to seek medical information from the referral source, which can make it easier for the physician to learn from us about psychosocial material. We become mutual students in the biopsychosocial understanding of the patient. We never have to prove ourselves as "real physicians," as do our psychiatric colleagues.

Referral Customs

Understanding referral customs is very important. In general, a hospital consultant does not provide feedback to a patient about results unless given permission to do so by the attending physician (which is usually easily obtained). In some hospitals, a psychologist should never see a patient unless it is requested by the attending physician, even if the nursing staff has requested help. However, good relationships with nursing staff are very important for a number of reasons: These staff members are frequently responsible for initiating consultations, they have valuable information to offer about the patient, and they are often critical to the intervention process.

In outpatient work, it is important to remember that one should never refer for consultation to a medical or dental colleague without going back to the original referral source (or family practitioner) to tactfully obtain his or her permission (we've never been denied). This is especially important in clinical health psychology, as the psychologist clinician constantly has to assess whether previous medical workups have been adequate, without having competence in that area. It is best to have established relationships with specialty practitioners in whom the clinician has a good deal of confidence. The clinical health psychologist will often obtain "curbside consultations" from these specialists and refer clients to them as patients, thus contributing to their practices.

An important aspect to keep in mind is that, when physicians request services from psychologists, they might actually feel somewhat threatened about admitting that they do not understand a patient or that they cannot handle a particular situation. This is probably more true when it comes to behavioral and emotional problems than when consultations are required of other specialists in medicine. In our culture, it appears that everyone, to some extent, considers herself or himself an expert in human relations. Breakdowns in interpersonal relationships are frequently blamed on the "other," but not without significant personal fears concerning one's own failure. So it is with health care providers and their patients, the result of which can be defensiveness or increased emotional reactivity on the part of the consultee. This needs to be handled with tact, not arrogance or condescending behavior that can exacerbate the problem. It is hypothesized that professional arrogance in psychologists is relatively more damaging to collaborative relationships with physicians, in part due to the nature of the problems being addressed, than would be arrogance displayed by another medical specialist (e.g., a cardiologist to a family practitioner). Indeed, we believe that there are a number of professional behaviors and personal attributes that can facilitate or hinder successful clinical health psychology practice.

SPECIAL ISSUES IN PROFESSIONAL BEHAVIOR

Another discipline often cannot judge the quality of psychological services, but physicians can judge whether such services are delivered in good professional style. Perhaps unfortunately, quality of care is often confused with quality of service, although the latter is certainly also important. However, style is frequently the only frame of reference from which the physician or the surgeon can judge, and the standards utilized are those of his or her own profession. Given this understanding, we suggest that the clinical health psychologist should (a) avoid overidentification with medicine, (b) fine-tune communication skills, (c) be prompt and follow through, (d) accept her or his limits of understanding, (e) be prepared for patient advocacy, and (f) advocate for quality services.

Avoid overidentification with medicine. Although there is a need to understand the health care system and to behave in a fashion that can earn credibility for the clinical health psychologist, it is also important to be aware of the potential for inappropriate medical socialization of clinical health psychologists. Elfant (1985) has articulated the traditional medical model, with its authoritarian stance and action orientation, and expressed his concerns that health psychology practitioners will overidentify with it. In doing so, they may forego the psychological treatment model that insists on autonomy and freedom of choice for both patient and therapist. As he states: "The fact that psychological assessment raises a multiplicity of hypotheses, issues and clinical guesses is disturbing news in the hospital environment where quick action is the norm" (p. 61). There are strong pressures in the health care system to come to bottom-line decisions—to "fix people". This is especially relevant to psychologists in the area of compliance with medical regimen, where the clinician must carefully evaluate who his or her client is, the health care system or the patient. We agree with Elfant that clinical health psychology must avoid the mistakes of the traditional medical model, which portrays the patient as sick and dependent and the professional as imperialistic and heroic.

Fine-tune communication skills. Suffice it to say that competence in the eyes of physicians will *not* be demonstrated through the use of psychological jargon, be it psychoanalytic or behavioral in orientation. The rule of thumb is to be *concrete, practical, brief,* and *succinct.* Recommendations should be relevant to the consultee's behavior. It is often said that the longer the report, the less likely it is to be read.

Be prompt and follow up. In hospitals, consultations must often be provided within 24 hours or less, with full reports available immediately. Many consultations require more than one contact. A frequent complaint about psychiatric service providers is that they "drop the ball" by rendering an opinion and then leaving the case to the attending physician to manage, without either specific directions or proper follow-up support.

Outpatient psychiatric services are sometimes accused of being "rabbit holes" for patients, who are thought to disappear after the referral is made. Often this is not the result of inattention to the patient's needs but of a lack of follow-through in communication back to the referral sources.

Accept limits of understanding. Every discipline has its limits of understanding. Clinical health psychologists must not overestimate or overstate the boundaries of knowledge. As psychologists attempt to prove themselves in medical settings, this might be tempting, but it is likely to be ill-fated. One needs to know and to accept the limits inherent in the state of psychological knowledge and therapeutic efficacies and to be able to ask for help or information when appropriate. The psychologist should not project the image of a general "fixer" of human behavior; rather, she or he should convey a more limited range of expertise. Lipowski (1967) described the physician's view of the psychiatrist as "a scientifically unsophisticated, medically ignorant, and impractical man, given to sweeping statements about other people's motives based on abstruse theories of questionable validity" (p. 158). For over 20 years he has called upon psychiatrists to contradict this image, a message never completely heeded by either psychiatrists or psychologists, given some of the consultation reports we have seen.

Be prepared for patient advocacy. A final issue has to do with patient advocacy. Often the clinical health psychologist finds herself or himself in a mediating role between the health care system and the patient, sometimes having to actively advocate for patient needs. For example, a previous psychiatric diagnosis can affect physicians' willingness to pursue medical evaluations. We remember well the case of a 45-year-old former alcoholic who complained of back pain and was considered a hypochondriac, but who was actually suffering from a recurrence of bowel cancer. Thorough documentation of the nature of the complaints, the lack of evidence for psychological mechanisms to explain the symptoms and several phone calls to the attending physician persuaded him to do a more extensive workup. As a result, the patient felt more "authenticated" and, through therapy, worked out her anger at care givers as she became increasingly dependent upon them until her death.

Setting-related issues can also be extremely important in patient advocacy. For example, it has been said that in an HMO, in which the patient has less autonomy and control than in fee-for-service health care, health care professionals have special obligations to advocate for the patient and to act as internal critics of unfair HMO policies or colleagues' practices.

Advocate for quality services. If the psychologist witnesses a violation of patient rights or an inappropriate standard of care, appropriate action must be taken. Psychologists must know the local professional mechanisms, chains of authority, and structures available to deal with such problems.

According to Keith-Spiegel and Koocher (1985), psychologists' ethical principles (APA, 1981) implicitly encourage whistle-blowing if other mechanisms fail to resolve the problem. However, such activity is not without personal and professional self-sacrifice and risk. Keith-Spiegel and Koocher have encouraged the use of questions developed by Nader and his colleagues (Nader, Petkas, & Blackwell, 1972) that could assist the clinical health psychologist with decision making concerning this issue.

1. Is my knowledge of the matter complete and accurate?
2. What are the objectionable practices, and what public interest do they harm?
3. How far should I, and can I go inside the organization with my concern or objection?
4. Will I be violating any rules by contacting outside parties and, if so, is whistle-blowing nevertheless justified?
5. Will I be violating any laws or ethical duties by *not* contacting external parties?
6. Once I have decided to act, what is the best way to blow the whistle — anonymously, overtly, by resignation prior to speaking out, or in some other way?
7. What will be the likely response from various sources — inside and outside the organization — to the whistle-blowing action?
8. What is expected to be achieved by whistle-blowing in this particular situation? (Nader et al., 1972; p. 6)

Many of these questions are also useful in determining for oneself how far one wants to go, either within a setting or within a profession, to resolve problems.

PERSONAL CHARACTERISTICS

Before undertaking work in clinical health psychology, it is important to review some of the personal issues we have found related to one's ability to adjust to practice in this area. There are some individuals who are just not suited to the work; thus, it is better to examine these issues early in the process of training. Because clinical health psychology is receiving increased attention, with some glamorization of the nature of the work, individuals might be drawn to the field for inappropriate reasons or with unrealistic expectations. Mismatches between personal characteristics and professional requirements are costly, in terms of both time spent and emotional well-being. We have seen mismatches result in early burnout and, in the worst cases, pervasive anger, resentment, and nihilistic thinking. These attitudes are not only damaging to the individual practitioner but can also reflect negatively on the field as a whole. Personal characteristics considered to be related to successful practice are listed next.

Understanding one's own stimulus value. It is important for the clinician to assess whether he or she has any striking peculiarities that could interfere with early establishment of rapport, as rapport must often be accomplished quickly in this field. Given the bad press mental health professionals have had in the past, the more "shrink like" individual could be at quite a disadvantage. When we think of the most successful clinical health psychologists we have known, both in training and in the field, the descriptors *active, engaging, open, direct, assertive,* and *energetic* come to mind. In a survey of Veteran's Administration physicians, Schenkenberg, Peterson, Wood, & DaBell (1981) found the following adjectives used to describe important qualities for a psychological consultant: pleasant, personable, friendly, compassionate, empathic, sensitive, interested, available, able to communicate effectively, cooperative, intelligent, open, perceptive and displaying common sense.

Possession of a high frustration tolerance. The clinical health psychologist must be a persevering, patient individual who, given the frustrations in the field, can get along on a very thin schedule of reinforcement. We believe this to be very basic to work in the area. One must be able to tolerate the fluctuation of interest by the medical community in behavioral and emotional components of health. Despite all the current focus on comprehensive medicine, it is still often lip service. Many physicians care little about the values psychologists hold most dear. Physicians can be ambivalent, hostile (covert or overt), or indifferent. An attitude of "benevolent skepticism" is welcomed. Physicians sometimes fail to carry out recommendations (about 30% of the time, according to Billowitz and Friedson, 1978–79), discharge patients before evaluation or treatment is completed, refer patients without adequate preparation, or fail to acknowledge the expertise of the psychologist (everyone is a "psychologist").

The stereotype is that of all the medical specialties, family practitioners, internal medicine physicians, and pediatricians are the most sympathetic to psychology, whereas surgeons are the least sympathetic. In our experience, there appears to be more than a grain of truth to these stereotypes. However, we have also known some extremely sensitive and psychologically minded surgeons and some callous pediatricians.

Clinicians need to respond nondefensively to what could be perceived to be an M.D. versus Ph.D. prejudice. As Shows (1976) has pointed out, psychologists' prejudices against the medical model (which they equate with medicine) can lead to a readiness to project conflict into almost any situation. When a defensive or aggressive stance is taken, it can make collaborative efforts difficult. As one becomes more sophisticated in the health care system, it becomes evident that some conflict is a natural, ongoing part of the system and that it also occurs among medical specialties.

In general, psychologists with strong needs for external validation and recognition are not likely to do well on a long-term basis; they soon become angry and resentful. Rather, we believe the work is more suitable if one is primarily motivated by internal belief systems and achievement needs. This is because the system often yields too little external reinforcement, or yields it on a variable interval schedule.

Avoidance of professional fanaticism. Although we indicated the importance of being motivated by internal beliefs and earlier mentioned the somewhat missionary zeal with which a number of us embraced the field, we believe it important to not be fanatical in our beliefs about the importance of the biopsychosocial model and to not be wedded to any single treatment technique. We have witnessed the suspension of critical thinking by a number of colleagues who threw themselves into the wellness movement or the biofeedback movement, only to suffer a loss of credibility when they could not deliver the results they had anticipated.

Tolerance for a demanding work schedule. This is especially true if inpatient work is involved. Much consultation work in the hospital setting is unpredictable, and the psychologist must be available on short notice. Follow-through is essential and must accommodate whatever else has already been schedule. The work is not leisurely. Pressures can mount, especially when, as is often the case, there are demands for immediate solutions to very complex problems. Of course, settings do vary, and there *are* some systems in which clinical health psychologists maintain very much of a 9:00–5:00 schedule, with few deviations even in hospital work. Scheduling in outpatient practices is much more under the control of the clinician.

Ability to deal comfortably with hostile or reluctant patients. Specific suggestions for handling hostile patients will be given in chapter 8, but it is noted here that clinical health psychologists frequently see patients who are upset about the referral and display indifference, if not outright antagonism, when meeting the clinician. This is sometimes due to poor preparation by the physician but most often to mind–body dualism, which is alive and well both in patients and physicians. Further, if the clinician has strong needs to see patients who are actively seeking psychological help, this would not be the best area of practice.

Ability to cope with diverse sets of data. The clinical health psychologist needs to be comfortable with diverse sets of data (biological, social, psychological) and to attempt to integrate these, while recognizing that no single theory of behavior provides an adequate conceptualization. The clinician must remain flexible in operating within a variety of conceptual models, depending upon the case. The clinical health psychologist must guard against being too easily intimidated by biological models, which are often presented as being more precise than they actually are, while being overly self-critical of the behavioral sciences.

Ability to work with the physically ill. Patients seen by the clinical health psychologist can be gravely ill, deformed, mutilated, disabled, or dying. A period of acclimation is needed as one struggles within oneself against such potential stressors as the sight of blood, the burn unit, the fears of chronic pain, and the acceptance of terminal illness. The clinician's reactions to the patient in these areas are critical. The colostomy or mastectomy patient who is concerned with body image and fears of unacceptability must not be treated with squeamishness. Yet it is easy to be distracted from addressing patient feelings and attitudes in the presence of massive physical changes, such as those found on a head and neck surgery service (Petrucci and Harwick, 1984).

Empathy for the health care providers' perspectives. It is important to be able to communicate respect for the consultee and her or his problem (e.g., a demanding or noncompliant patient). Collaboration with medicine requires empathy not just in the evaluation of the patient, but also in dealing with the referral sources. The clinician needs to understand consultees' thinking styles and perspectives on patient care. This requires in-depth understanding of the roles, functions, and stressors in various hospital units and outpatient clinics. This is perhaps best obtained via naturalistic observation.

Acceptance of dependence upon another profession. Psychology is an independent profession, but the practice of clinical health psychology has aspects of a forced dependency upon the expertise and performance of another profession, usually medicine or dentistry. Some psychologists we have known have had special difficulty with this forced dependency, especially when it involved a profession of greater social status.

Appropriateness as a health model. Weiss (1982), in his 1980 Presidential Address to the Division of Health Psychology, highlighted the importance of health psychologists' assessing their personal suitability as role models. The clinical health psychologist should be aware of personal habits such as smoking, obesity, alcohol usage, and physical fitness. Modeling of appropriate personal health behavior is related not only to therapeutic effectiveness, if one adopts a social learning theory model, but also to ethical principles, as will be discussed in chapter 4.

In summary, beyond obtaining the core body of clinical health psychology knowledge, preparation to become an effective clinical health psychologist requires attention to a broad range of professional and personal issues.

SUGGESTED READINGS

American Psychological Association. (1985). *A Hospital practice primer for psychologists.* Washington, DC: Author.

Binner, P. R. (1986) DRG's and the administration of mental health services. *American Psychologist, 41,* 64–69.

Lipowski, Z. J. (1967). Review of consultation psychiatry and psychosomatic medicine: I. General principles, *Psychosomatic Medicine, 29,* 153–171.

Stricker, G. (1983). Peer review systems in psychology. In B. D. Sales (Ed.), *The professional psychologists' handbook.* New York: Plenum.

Chapter 4

Ethical Issues in the Practice of Clinical Health Psychology

The practice of clinical health psychology brings with it unique ethical issues due to the special settings and patient populations encountered, although the *Ethical Principles of Psychologists* (APA, 1981) are of course applicable. This chapter examines the first eight of these principles: (a) Responsibility, (b) Competence, (c) Moral and Legal Standards, (d) Public Statements, (e) Confidentiality, (f) Welfare of the Consumer, (g) Professional Relationships, and (h) Assessment Techniques (APA, 1981, p. 633–638). The principles of Research with Human Participants and Care and Use of Animals were excluded as not relevant to our focus on clinical practice. The following discussion derives from an examination of the subparagraphs of each ethical principle and the *Standards for Providers of Psychological Services* (APA, 1985c). The reader is referred to the original sources for complete documentation.

PRINCIPLE 1. RESPONSIBILITY

In providing services, psychologists maintain the highest standards of their profession. They accept responsibility for the consequences of their acts and make every effort to ensure that their services are used appropriately. (p. 633)

This standard subsumes many of the subsequent ethical principles. Subparagraphs specify that this responsibility extends to personal, social, organizational, financial, and political involvements. For the clinical health psychologist, the principle of responsibility includes issues of quality assurance, increased responsibility for physical health, and the risk of diffusion of responsibility for aspects of patient care in a large health care institution.

Responsibility, Accountability, and Quality Assurance

There are three basic rights that determine the integrity of an independent profession (D. F. Jacobs, 1983):

1. Self-determination of the qualifications of candidates for entry into the profession
2. Autonomy of professional functioning within the bounds established by social, moral, and legal responsibilities
3. Self-regulation, exercised through peer review and based on a self-promulgated code of ethics, as well as self-promulgated standards of practice (p. 20)

For psychologists, these aspects are reflected in the *Standards for Providers of Psychological Services* (APA, 1985c) and the *Ethical Principles of Psychologists* (APA, 1981). More specifically, the ethical principles of *responsibility* and *welfare of the consumer* and the standard of *accountability* mandate the assurance of quality services. As part of this directive, psychologists must engage in quality assessment (a measurement of quality of care; Stricker, 1983) in which peer review and accountability are essential elements:

(3.1) Psychologists' professional activity shall be primarily guided by the principle of promoting human welfare.
(3.3) There shall be periodic, systematic, and effective evaluations of psychological services.
(3.4) Psychologists are accountable for all aspects of services they provide and shall be responsible to those concerned with services. (APA, 1985c)

Clinical health psychologists are governed by the same principles as those in general practice; thus it is essential that the psychologist obtain periodic review of his or her services. If one is working in a larger health care institution, peer review systems are often already in place, as they are a basic requirement for accreditation by the JCAH. Models of peer review can differ, so long as the goal of quality assurance is achieved (see Miller, 1981).

As an example, in a large health care organization with which we are familiar, a multidisciplinary peer review committee monitors mental health services. Membership on the committee rotates at regular intervals. All mental health staff members are required to submit to periodic chart review of cases. Feedback is provided by the committee, with appearances by the professional required as necessary. Cases are selected in a somewhat random fashion: the committee chooses an arbitrary date and requires the clinician to submit the first appointment seen or new case opened. This chart is reviewed in terms of assessment, diagnostic formulation, and treatment plan. Other considerations include documentation of treatment and relevant legal and ethical issues. The peer review committee is completely separate from administrative structures (although department administration also reviews a random sample of clinicians' charts on an annual basis). In another institution, a weekly case conference is held to allow faculty to present their own clinical cases for peer review, critique, and discussion in a group setting.

It is important for the clinical health psychologist that the reviewer is qualified to assess the particular services delivered. For example, the child clinical therapist might not be competent to provide adequate peer review of a clinical health psychologist working on a coronary care unit, and vice versa. The psychologist must work toward developing a competent review of her or his services.

The clinical health psychologist in independent practice has a difficult time obtaining adequate peer review. Although there is nationwide peer review of services offered by psychologists built into many third-party payment systems (see Stricker, 1983; Stricker & Cohen, 1984; Theaman, 1984), these offer only cursory assessment of treatment, often guided primarily by insurance-reimbursement policies. It can be useful to begin study groups or to contract for mutual peer review with colleagues in the community. This not only provides for quality assurance but also increases the probability that one is practicing in accordance with prevailing community standards. (See chapter 5 for a discussion of malpractice issues.)

Responsibility for Physical Health

One unique aspect of clinical health psychology is increased responsibility for physical health (Swencionis, Hall, & Macklen, in press). More so than in traditional practice, the clinical health psychologist deals with psychological factors associated with medical conditions. Therefore, such things as concomitant medical evaluation and management must be assured. The clinical health psychologist also more often interfaces with the medical system, both on an individual and an institutional level. This interaction can be intimately tied to patient care (for instance, being sure a particular medical evaluation is completed or helping a patient confront health care system problems). To successfully assume this responsibility for patient care, we have found that one must have many of the personal attributes discussed in chapter 2.

Risk of Diffusion of Responsibility

Another area relevant to the responsible practice of clinical health psychology is what Zerubavel (1980) called the "bureaucratization of responsibility." He held that within the hospital context there is ever-increasing segmentation of responsibility for patients. Hospital patients are cared for by a myriad of specialized clinicians. Thus, the responsibility for the patient does not lie with any one clinician but rather with a collective entity such as "the hospital" or "the team." (As Zerubavel pointed out, the legal responsibility for the patient lies ultimately with the attending physician.) With such a complex organizational structure, the likelihood of diffusion of responsibility or *floating responsibility* becomes very great. Under these conditions, passivity on the part of the clinical health psychologist can go unnoticed, because so many aspects of care are occurring simultaneously. For example, such things as treatment planning, record keeping, follow-up, communication with other professionals, and informed consent might not be responsibly completed. The psychologist must take care to provide responsible care to patients even when the structure of the system allows for diffusion of responsibility or passivity. Issues of patient advocacy are addressed more specifically in chapter 3.

PRINCIPLE 2. COMPETENCE

The maintenance of high standards of competence is a responsibility shared by all psychologists in the interest of the public and the profession as a whole. Psychologists recognize the boundaries of their competence and the limitations of their technique. They only provide services and only use the techniques for which they are qualified by training and experience. In those areas in which recognized standards do not yet exist, psychologists take whatever precautions are necessary to protect the welfare of their clients. They maintain knowledge of current scientific and professional information related to the services they render. (p. 634)

Issues particularly relevant to clinical health psychology are competence in training, recognition of boundaries of competence, maintenance of current knowledge, work with people of different backgrounds, and recognition of personal problems that might interfere with practice.

Competence in Training

Since the Arden House Conference (see chapter 2), guidelines have been established for training practitioners in health psychology. Of course, these are ideals at present; many of the senior health psychologists today do not have such a training background themselves. Even so, it is well recognized that weekend workshops do not produce a clinical health psychologist. As discussed in detail in chapter 2, core training and preparation for clinical health psychology practice should include specific graduate-level courses in the area and supervised practical experience. A psychologist should not present himself or herself as a clinical health psychologist unless training criteria have been adequately satisfied.

Recognition of One's Boundaries of Competence

A psychologist must insure the best interests and welfare of the patient who presents with a problem of psychological factors related to a medical problem. Consider the following example:

> Dr. Smith, a clinical psychologist, worked in a private practice setting serving mostly adults. In the course of her work, she began therapy with a 22-year-old male who had been suffering from muscle contraction headaches. Dr. Smith had done some reading about the treatment of muscle contraction headaches, but had never actually treated an individual with this problem. She continued treating the individual, but received supervision from a clinical health psychologist experienced in the treatment of chronic headaches.

Dr. Smith acted appropriately and ethically in this example. Had she not received the outside supervision, she could have been acting unethically in not "obtaining training, experience, or counsel to assure competent service" (Principle 2d). This is especially true in cases of psychophysiological disorders, as there are often clearly specified and empirically validated treatment approaches available for use. Another option might had been for the psychologist to have referred the patient to a colleague for concurrent treatment of the headache problem (although cross consultation is not as frequent in psychology as it is in medicine).

A related issue arises from the fact that a psychologist is unlikely to be proficient in all the areas of practice that fall into the field of clinical health psychology. As indicated in chapter 1, clinical health psychology includes such diverse problems as eating disorders and headaches, as well as such diverse assessments as neuropsychological evaluations and chronic pain patient workups. The skills necessary for these different clinical tasks are extremely varied. As noted, the clinical health psychologist must be aware of her or his limitations, even within the field, and take steps to assure ethical professional behavior.

Maintenance of Current Knowledge

In a field as rapidly changing as clinical health psychology, it is essential to keep abreast of current literature. Attending continuing education workshops, belonging to professional organizations, and subscribing to health psychology journals can facilitate this. It has been said that the half-life of a PhD in clinical psychology is only about 10 years if no further postgraduate education is sought (Dubin, 1972). In the area of clinical health psychology, this estimate may be too generous, due to the high level of research and clinical activity.

Work with People of Different Backgrounds

Ethical principle 2d states that, "Psychologists recognize differences among people, such as those that may be associated with age, sex, socioeconomic, and ethnic backgrounds." Although we know of no data on this, it could be that clinical health psychology patient populations represent more of a cross section of society than the populations presenting for services at "mental health" clinics. We find that to meet this ethical guideline in the practice of clinical health psychology, an understanding of patients' health belief models is essential. Further, it is important to appreciate the cultural and other factors that influence patients' explanatory frameworks for medical problems. The following is an overview of a conceptual model useful in accomplishing these goals.

A conceptual distinction among *disease, illness,* and *sickness* is helpful in understanding patients presenting to clinical health psychologists (Engel, 1977; Fabrega, 1974; Kleinman, Eisenberg, & Good, 1977). *Disease* is an abnormality in physical structure or bodily function; it is the focus of biomedicine. *Illness,* on the other hand, is the "human experience of sickness" and is influenced by interpersonal, social, and cultural variables (Mechanic, 1972). Illness entails our explanation of the disease and how we think we are supposed to act when we are ill. It is how we perceive, experience, and cope with disease. Consistent with this model, there is rarely a one-to-one relationship between disease and illness (Beecher, 1956; Melzack & Wall, 1983). The combined influences of disease and illness yield what we ultimately observe clinically as *sickness.* Patients are generally much more concerned with the treatment of their *illness* than simply with the cure of the disease.

Ethical principle 2d dictates that the clinical health psychologist have an understanding of this model. The domain of clinical health psychology treatment often encompasses illness behavior, explanatory beliefs, and sickness. When there is a significant discrepancy between the doctor's and the patient's explanatory models, problems in treatment can occur.

Mrs. A. B. was a 56-year-old Caucasian woman who was recovering, on a general medical unit, from pulmonary edema secondary to atherosclerotic cardiovascular disease and chronic congestive heart failure. Her physical status was improving, but she frequently induced vomiting and urinated into her bed. She became very angry when told by the staff to stop these behaviors. Psychological consultation revealed that the patient had been told by her physician that part of her medical problem included water in the lungs. Because of her family's occupation—most were plumbers—her conception of her anatomy consisted of a pipe connecting her mouth and her urethra. She was therefore attempting to remove as much water from her body as possible via vomiting and urinating. She was hesitant to share this belief model with her physician because "he was so rushed" and she felt embarrassed. A sharing of the doctor's and the patient's explanatory models, including a careful didactic session about her anatomy, resulted in a resolution of the problem behaviors and feelings of anger. (Adapted from Kleinman et al., 1977)

Other common examples of patients' misconceptions about medical treatments include the ideas that (a) if one pill is good, two or more must be better; (b) if symptoms are not occurring, the pills are not necessary (often seen in the usage of medication for hypertension and diabetes); and (c) continued use of *any* medication is "overdependence." As can be seen, any of these beliefs can have serious consequences for medical treatment.

Kleinman et al. (1977) suggested that, when addressing a patient's belief model, one should attempt to (a) elicit the patient's belief model with simple, straightforward questions; (b) formulate the physician's model in terms the patient can understand and communicate this to the patient; (c) openly compare models to identify contradictions; and (d) help the physician and the patient engage in a negotiation toward shared models related to treatment and outcome. Awareness of cultural and social issues related to a patient's belief model is crucial in guiding this process. It must also be realized that subgroups other than identified minority cultures can have beliefs about illness that affect behavior (as portrayed in the example). It could be unethical to fail to address these issues.

Recognition of Personal Problems.

Ethical principle 2f dictates that psychologists be aware of personal problems that might interfere with professional effectiveness and take appropriate measures to prevent harm. If such problems arise, the psychologist is to seek professional consultation to evaluate whether practice should be limited, suspended, or terminated. For example, the clinical health psychologist with significant concerns in the areas of death, anxiety, or body image might not be able to work effectively with, or might do actual harm to, certain medical–surgical patients (e.g., through communication of revulsion at the sight of a postmastectomy patient).

PRINCIPLE 3. MORAL AND LEGAL STANDARDS

Psychologists' moral and ethical standards of behavior are a personal matter to the same degree as they are for any other citizen, except as these may compromise the fulfillment of their professional responsibilities or reduce the public trust in psychology and psychologists. Regarding their own behavior, psychologists are sensitive to prevailing community standards and to the possible impact that conformity or deviation from these standards may have upon the quality of their performance as psychologists. Psychologists are also aware of the possible impact of their public behavior upon the ability of colleagues to perform their professional duties. (p. 639)

Principle 3 deals with at least two unique issues in the practice of clinical health psychology. These are one's personal behavior as it relates to one's profession as a psychologist and the imposition of values on the patient.

Personal Behavior

The clinical health psychologist could have to meet standards of behavior beyond those inherent in general psychological practice. As an extreme example, the clinician who is a heavy smoker, is very overweight, drinks an excessive amount of coffee, and consumes more than a moderate amount of alcohol often has special problems in relationships with professional colleagues (physicians and psychologists) as well as patients, and may have difficulty in representing health psychology to the public. Although this could appear to be an infringement on one's personal freedom of choice, Principle 3 states clearly that personal behavior can come under ethical scrutiny when it affects professional practice. The clinical health psychologist must be aware of personal health habits and make decisions about acceptable, ethical public behavior. These behaviors cannot be rigidly defined, nor should they be, but rather a range of acceptable behaviors must be decided upon individually.

Imposition of Values on the Patient

Extending moral and legal standards to the treatment of patients, the clinical health psychologist is not justified in imposing rigid criteria for "healthy behaviors" on patients. Working within the patient's health belief model and expectations for treatment is necessary to the formulation of treatment goals. For example, the Mexican–American patient who suffers from ulcers might be willing to modify a formerly spicy diet but might outrightly reject an admonition to switch to bland food. The clinical health psychologist could be doing an injustice by holding to the latter treatment goal, thus not only risking treatment failure but also decreasing the probability that future intervention would be successful.

PRINCIPLE 4. PUBLIC STATEMENTS

Public statements, announcements of services, advertising, and promotional activities of psychologists serve the purpose of helping the public make informed judgments and choices. Psychologists represent accurately and objectively their qualifications, affiliations, and functions, as well as those of the institutions or organizations with which they or the statements may be associated. In public statements providing psychological information about the availability of psychological products, publications, and services, psychologists base their statements on scientifically acceptable psychological findings and techniques with full recognition of the limits and uncertainties of such evidence. (pp. 634–635)

The primary focus of this ethical principle involves two facets: advertising one's own services and endorsements for psychological services or related products.

Advertising One's own Services

Advertising by psychologists may contain such information as "name, highest relevant academic degree earned from a regionally accredited institution, date, type and level of certification or licensure, diplomate status, APA membership status, services offered, fee information, foreign languages spoken, and policy with regard to third-party payments" (Principle 4a).

The clinical health psychologist might include in advertising that he or she specializes in the treatment of psychological issues related to health problems or a particular subcategory of practice (e.g., chronic headaches, stress disorders, eating disorders, smoking cessation). Because the Federal Trade Commission has loosened guidelines on professional advertising, most simple factual information about one's services is probably reasonable (Koocher, 1983). What is prohibited in advertising are testimonials, evaluative comments regarding one's treatment success, or exaggeration of the uniqueness of services offered. Unwarranted claims — such as "Hypnotherapy will end smoking and overeating in one day," or "Ten sessions of biofeedback will eliminate your headache problem" — would be considered unfounded and unethical.

Endorsements

Beyond advertising for one's own services, care must be taken in the endorsement of products or printed materials. In clinical health psychology there has been an explosion of practice-related technology such as relaxation tapes, hypnosis tapes, self-help manuals, and biofeedback equipment. Sensational claims related to the efficacy of these procedures might include such statements as

In this manual you will learn to subliminally reprogram yourself to lose weight, eliminate pain, and quit smoking in a short amount of time using these proven audiotapes.

These tapes will produce positive restructuring of self-image, alleviate depression, and increase self-esteem.

These relaxation methods have been proven to inhibit postoperative swelling, pain, and bleeding, and to produce rapid healing. They are also used for all pain management.

The real cause of smoking is stress, and you'll learn to control it through this proven and tested home biofeedback system.

These hypothetical statements can be considered sensational and unethical, as they go beyond what has been validated. Further, they do not specify the context within which these techniques have been tested (e.g., as used in a comprehensive psychological treatment package). The psychologist is ethically bound to protect how her or his name is used, even when production or publication rights have been transferred to a marketing company.

PRINCIPLE 5. CONFIDENTIALITY

Psychologists have a primary obligation to respect the confidentiality of information obtained from persons in the course of their work as psychologists. They reveal such information to others only with the consent of the person or the person's legal representative, except in those unusual circumstances in which not to do so would result in clear danger to the person or to others. Where appropriate, psychologists inform their clients of the legal limits of confidentiality. (p. 636)

Privileged versus Confidential Information

Privileged communication refers to the legal confidentiality between psychologist and patient. The limits of this privilege are determined by state statutes and vary from state to state. The "privilege" of confidentiality lies with the patient, and, except in special circumstances, the psychologist must abide by the patient's determination.

Confidentiality is an ethical concept, but it is influenced by legal guidelines (such as mandates to breach confidentiality to prevent self-harm or harm to others; see chapter 5). The psychologist must maintain a confidential relationship with the patient and obtain permission before releasing information.

Special Confidentiality Problems in Clinical Health Psychology

Chapter 5 discusses some of the special confidentiality problems in clinical health psychology including providing information to the referral source, charting treatment notes in a widely circulated medical record rather than a less-available psychological record, and the release of medical records containing psychological treatment notes to an outside source. Other problems arise in providing services to multiple-bed hospital rooms, discussing cases within the context of a multidisciplinary team approach, and discussion of the patient's psychological status with members of the patient's family.

Generally, the clinical health psychologist should strive to maximize confidentiality. One should also inform the patient of the limits of confidentiality, as set both by law and by institutional organization. For instance, finding a setting to conduct confidential psychological services on a medical–surgical unit can be very difficult. Patient consultation rooms are sometimes available, but these are often heavily scheduled. If the patient is nonambulatory and is in a multiple-bed room, it might not be possible to maintain confidentiality (unless services can be scheduled when other patients are out of the room). The patient should be explicitly given the option of declining services if not comfortable with the situation; otherwise, the pressure from an "authoritative" professional could induce the patient to engage in behavior without true consent. Similarly, when a patient's psychological status is to be discussed in the context of a team treatment approach, the patient should be informed of what material will be discussed. Last, we have found that pressure from family members to discuss the patient's psychological status often arises in cases of brain dysfunction, "conversion" disorders, and compliance problems that can be closely related to family-system issues (e.g., eating disorders, compliance with insulin treatment regimens, chronic pain management). If the patient is not able to make informed decisions, such as in brain dysfunction cases, legal and ethical guidelines may allow release of confidential information to an appointed person as necessary. Except in these instances, the process of obtaining a written release of confidential information should be followed, as in any traditional psychological case.

PRINCIPLE 6. WELFARE OF THE CONSUMER

Psychologists respect the integrity and protect the welfare of the people and groups with whom they work. When conflicts of interest arise between clients and psychologists' employing institutions, psychologists clarify the nature and direction of their loyalties and responsibilities and keep all parties informed of their commitments. Psychologists fully inform consumers as to the purpose and nature of an evaluative, treatment, educational, or training procedure, and they freely acknowledge that clients, students, or participants in research have freedom of choice with regard to participation. (p. 636)

The primary purpose of Principle 6 is to safeguard consumers of psychological services against exploitation. The psychologist must be aware of such issues as informed consent, conflicts of interest between treatment of the patient and employing institutions, provision of services at the request of a third party, and patients who do not benefit from treatment.

Informed Consent

The doctrine of informed consent was developed so that patients could weigh the risks and benefits of a treatment and determine for themselves if they wanted to participate (Barton & Sanborn, 1978; Knapp & VandeCreek, 1981). The patient should understand the nature of the proposed treatment, the risks and likelihood of success, and the available alternative treatments. Ideally, the procedure of informed consent is meant to force the health care professional to make the patient more of an equal bargaining partner in treatment decisions (Stone, A. A., 1979). There has been an increase in interest in informed consent for medical and psychological treatments with the consumerism movement among patients and judicial involvement in this area (Widiger & Rorer, 1984).

The legal concept of informed consent includes capacity, information, and voluntariness. *Capacity* means that a patient must have the ability to make rational decisions (this tenet often excludes children and the developmentally disabled from being able to give informed consent and necessitates proxy consent by a guardian). *Information* consists of both the substance of the material presented and the manner in which it is given. It is gauged by demonstrated understanding by the patient. *Voluntariness* refers to the fact that the patient is able to exercise free choice, without coercion, in making the decision.

Obtaining consent on the basis of inadequate information is unethical, and has been grounds for malpractice in medicine (Cohen & Mariano, 1982). A significant problem is how much to actually disclose about treatment (Halperin, 1980; Schutz, 1982). Adequate disclosure is legally determined by the community standard (telling patients what other practitioners in the community would tell their patients under similar circumstances) and "the reasonable person" statute (telling the patient what a reasonable person would need to know in order to make an informed decision). However, these guidelines actually offer the practitioner little guidance (Stone, A. A., 1979).

Other problems are revealed by the fact that informed consent procedures are often inadequate when patient understanding and retention of material are assessed (see Ley, 1982, for review). Such problems are sometimes related to readability of consent forms. For example, Grunder

(1980) analyzed five surgical consent forms from major Eastern hospitals and found that each was written at the upper undergraduate or graduate level of language; four of the five were at the level of a scientific journal. In addition, it has been found that, although a majority of patients have reported that "just the right amount" of information has been given, they often remember very little (Cassileth, Zupkis, Sutton-Smith, & March, 1980). Research findings in this area present serious problems for the practitioner in obtaining informed consent. Because of legal pressures, many medical professionals have gone to what might be considered the extreme position of providing all possible risks in graphic detail to ensure completeness. Problems with this approach and suggestions for a process of informed consent will be discussed later.

Clinical health psychologists could be involved in several aspects of informed consent in the medical setting. In our work, we are often involved in (a) helping the physician to explore the patient's health belief model about aspects of treatment and to determine the extent of the patient's understanding or possible misconceptions; (b) working with patients to encourage behaviors that will increase the likelihood of "true" informed consent (including determining what specific questions the patient has about the medical treatment and teaching the patient how to obtain information from the physician); and (c) helping patients deal with the increased feelings of uncertainty about treatment that often occur after the explicit informed consent procedures are carried out.

Clinical health psychologists must also deal with the issue of informed consent in the course of delivery of psychological services. Many practitioners view informed consent with contempt, and rarely provider information about alternate treatments. Gutheil, Bursztajn, Hamm, & Brodsky (1983) have suggested that the informed consent process is a double-edged sword. The positive aspect is that it clarifies options and stimulates understanding. The negative aspect is that it can increase the patient's uncertainty about treatment and decrease belief in the doctor's ability to cure. We agree with Gutheil et al. (1983) that the informed consent procedure should be entered into as a process of mutual discovery rather than as a formality. We outline the rationale for service, treatment plan, and goals in an atmosphere of open negotiation. Once a plan is formulated, it is useful to have the patient paraphrase his or her understanding of the evaluation or treatment so that misperceptions can be corrected.

We have found that the process of informed consent can often be difficult with patients referred to a clinical health psychologist. Often the physician has given the patient inadequate or incorrect information about our services. Further, the patient is now expected to shift from a biomedical to a biopsychosocial orientation. Overwhelming the patient in the first session with details of a treatment plan and expectations can result in premature termination. The informed consent procedure can extend over many sessions—in fact, over the entire course of treatment. Utilizing skills in working with people of different backgrounds (Competency) facilitates the informed consent process.

Conflicts of Interest

When dealing with the medical system, conflicts of interest can arise. There can occur a basic, unacknowledged, antagonistic relationship between patient and hospital or employee of the institution (Bazelon, 1974). As Noll stated, "Whenever the mental health professional is employed by an agency or by an institution, the institution needs will almost invariably supercede those of the patient" (1976, p. 1451). Thus, the clinical health psychologist might have a "hidden agenda" when consulting to a medical–surgical unit, depending on the needs of the staff and the reason for the consultation request.

> The patient was a 37-year-old, married Caucasian female who had been diagnosed as having lung cancer with multiple metastases. The prognosis was very poor. She had been through several courses of chemotherapy without significant benefit. A more experimental drug had been suggested, but the patient refused, stating she would rather be discharged to home. A referral for psychological evaluation of the patient's mental status was made. When the clinical health psychologist arrived on the unit, it was verbally communicated to her by the staff that "the patient needs to be convinced to stay in the hospital for further treatment, as it is her only hope of survival." The psychological evaluation revealed that the patient had carefully considered her options in treatment, was fully informed about risks and benefits of each alternative, and had made a decision with a clear sensorium and intact mental status. The psychologist reported the results of her evaluation to the staff and subsequently dealt with the anger and frustration of staff toward both her and the patient.

In this example, the psychologist might have easily been influenced by staff issues and spoken with the patient with the goal of convincing her to have the experimental treatment. Psychologists must remember to be responsible to the patient, to take into account the needs of the patient rather than those of the staff, and to "clarify the nature and direction of their loyalties and responsibilities and keep all parties informed of commitments" (Principle 6).

Services at the Request of a Third Party

The services of a clinical health psychologist are often requested by a physician to provide evaluation, treatment, or both. The psychologist must always determine the extent of the patient's understanding of why the consultation was requested and whether services are actually necessary. We find that many times the physician has not told the patient a consultation had been ordered; informed consent must be acquired before proceeding.

Further, many consultation requests are found to result from projection on the part of providers who are experiencing frustration, anger, depression, or some other emotional response to the patient (see chapters 6 and 8 for more discussion of these issues). Intervention is sometimes more appropriately targeted at the staff than the patient. A thorny ethical problem then arises: how to determine who is going to pay for the staff intervention? Is time billed to the patient?

Other areas where the services of a clinical health psychologist are often requested by a third party include neuropsychological assessment, psychological evaluation for a specific treatment program or procedure, and evaluation required when filing a Workmen's Compensation or disability claim. Patients are often not aware that when requesting some of these insurance programs to pay for services, they must agree to release their psychological evaluations as conditions of reimbursement. In any of these situations, the psychologist must fully inform the patient as to the nature and purpose of the assessment, what the results will be used for, who requested the evaluation, and who will pay for it (Cross & Deardorff, 1987; see also chapter 6).

Patients Who Do Not Benefit from Treatment

If a patient does not benefit from treatment after a reasonable trial, the psychologist is ethically mandated to terminate the treatment and to help with an appropriate referral. The clinical health psychologist often receives referrals that are "last-option" cases, in that all previous traditional medical treatments have failed (e.g., chronic pain syndromes, tinnitus, blepharospasm, atypical facial pain). In these cases, the psychological referral is to "give it a try," as there appear to be no other options. These cases represent clinical challenges in which the therapist must gauge carefully, in realistic negotiation with the patient, when an adequate trial of treatment has been undergone without significant benefit. The following case illustrates such a decision:

> The patient was a 78-year-old married Caucasian female with a postherpetic neuralgia secondary to having herpes zoster several years prior. The pain, as well as an excoriated skin surface, was distributed in a dermatomal pattern on the right side of the face and neck. Extensive dermatological treatments had failed to provide relief, and the patient was referred for pain management. Evaluation indicated that the symptoms did fluctuate, with stress and tension being related to an exacerbation of the condition and relaxed states being associated with symptom relief. A treatment plan was

formulated that included relaxation training with suggestions for hypnotic analgesia. After the patient had gained the ability to relax across all settings and practiced routinely with autohypnosis, no pain relief, as documented by symptom charting, had occurred. It was decided that the patient would not benefit from further treatment with that therapist and that an adequate trial had been given. The patient was referred for evaluation for trial of an antidepressant and phenothiazine combination (found useful in some cases by Loeser [1986]). She was also given a referral to another psychologist experienced in hypnotic analgesia, to see whether a different approach might be beneficial.

In this example the psychologist had to make a decision, with the patient's full participation, as to when an adequate trial had been attempted. The psychologist must also provide a referral if other treatments are available. The termination process in these cases must be handled carefully, so that the patient is not left with a failure experience (to prevent iatrogenic deterioration effects due to the treatment) but can capitalize on the positive effects, however small, of the treatment.

PRINCIPLE 7. PROFESSIONAL RELATIONSHIPS

Psychologists act with due respect for the needs, special competencies, and obligations of their colleagues in psychology and other professions. They respect the perogatives and obligations of the institutions or organizations with which these other colleagues are associated (p. 636)

As indicated, patient care in both inpatient and outpatient settings is often provided by multiple clinicians of varying specialties. The psychologist usually provides only one aspect of the complete treatment package. It is imperative that regular communication occur among professionals. This is often achieved in team meetings but many times is accomplished chiefly through chart notes. One of the most common complaints we hear from our physician colleagues is that they have referred to a psychologist (or other type of clinician) and receive no feedback on the evaluation or course of treatment. It is helpful to maintain written as well as verbal contact with other professionals to be sure treatments are coordinated in an appropriate manner.

Enhancement of professional relationships, as well as good patient care, are facilitated by a working knowledge of the roles of other professions. For instance, on any one case there could be a surgeon, an infectious disease physician, a nutritionist, a physical therapist, nursing staff, and a clinical health psychologist. An understanding of what each profession does helps the psychologist communicate more effectively, gain respect, and be aware of any treatment needs of the patient that are not being adequately met. It is also important to be aware of the varying ethical principles by which different professions abide.

PRINCIPLE 8. ASSESSMENT TECHNIQUES

In the development, publication, and utilization of psychological assessment techniques, psychologists make every effort to guard the welfare and best interests of the client. They respect the client's right to know the results, the interpretations made, and bases for their conclusions and recommendations. Psychologists make every effort to maintain the security of tests and other assessment techniques within the limits of legal mandates. They strive to ensure the appropriate use of assessment techniques by others. (p. 637)

In the psychological assessment of medical patients, the clinical health psychologist must be acutely aware of the proper standardization data for medical patients when available; differences in test interpretation with a medical–surgical patient population, rather than a psychiatric population; increased risk of inappropriate use of test results by nonpsychologist health care professionals; the language of the test interpretation and risk of misinterpretation; and systemic issues hampering the patient's right to be informed of the test results. Consider the following relatively common example:

The patient was a 34-year-old, married Caucasian female who presented to her primary physician with diffuse and vague somatic complaints, including pain. The patient also said that she had recently been experiencing some significant life stressors, and the physician hypothesized that these might be contributory. Initial physical evaluation was negative, which was consistent with the physician's hypothesis, and the patient was referred for psychological evaluation including psychological testing. The consultation request was to "determine if the symptoms might have a functional rather than organic basis." On the Minnesota Multiphasic Personality Inventory (MMPI), scored using standard normative data, the patient obtained a classic *conversion V* profile, with scales one and three primed and all other scales below a *T* score of 70.

The psychologist gave the following interpretation of the MMPI and sent the recommendations to the physician without discussing them with the patient. Informed consent had been obtained to release the test results to the physician.

Patients with similar profiles present themselves as normal, responsible, and without fault. They make extensive use of such defenses as projection, denial, and rationalization and blame others for their troubles. They prefer medical explanations for their symptoms, lacking insight into the psychological basis for them. These patients are generally considered to be converting personally distressing problems into somatic complaints, which are more socially acceptable. Although these patients are resistant to change due to firmly entrenched defense systems, a course of psychotherapy targeting the patient's actual source of distress might be useful. (Based on Graham, 1977; Greene, 1980).

The physician referred the patient for psychological treatment on the basis of the earlier evaluation. The psychological treatment was successful in resolving the stressful life circumstances with which the patient was having trouble, but the physical symptoms persisted. The patient was ultimately diagnosed as having multiple sclerosis, following further diagnostic work including magnetic resonance imaging.

This example illustrates a major ethical issue related to psychological assessment in health psychology. The psychologist used standard normative data to derive the patient's profile. Although this can be adequate if the use of such norms is taken into account in the interpretation, a more useful approach would be to use both the standard norms and those for medical patients (either norms generated in one's own clinic or those published in the literature such as Greene, 1980) and to compare the differences.

Other issues in this example, and more important ones as they influenced the course of the patient's treatment, are the consultation request itself and the interpretation of the results. *First,* the physician requested an inappropriate use for psychological testing. Although this type of request is commonly received from medical personnel, recent reviews of the literature suggest that psychologists who use the MMPI to assess pain patients should "not attempt to classify patients as organic, functional, or mixed" (Prokop & Bradley, 1981, p. 96). *Second,* the psychologist used a standard interpretation developed on psychiatric patients. This included conjecture as to the etiology of the physical symptoms and several personality labels that might be cast as pejorative by a non-mental-health professional.

Another problem with the response to this referral was that the language of the interpretation might not be considered consistent with ethically "guarding against the misuse of assessment results" and promoting the "best interests of the client." Without further explanation, the physician could well change her or his opinion of this patient and tend to see the patient as somehow volitionally controlling the presentation of symptoms or consciously malingering, although no evidence suggested this.

The last ethical issue related to this case is that the results of the assessment were not discussed directly with the patient by the psychologist. This should always be done, as discussed in more detail in chapters 5 and 6.

In summary, in this case, the test results were not utilized in the best interests of the patient. Even if the patient had not ultimately been found to have multiple sclerosis, psychological evaluation should rarely preclude thorough medical evaluation. Exceptions to this guideline might include such extreme cases as somatic delusions or factitious disorders where there is a history of unnecessary extensive medical evaluations and procedures.

Clinical health psychologists must be aware of special psychological assessment issues in working with medical patients, as general-practice assessment skills are not always applicable. When the psychologist is not familiar with current literature in the area, he or she is at higher risk of unethical practice. A complete discussion of assessment issues in health psychology can be found in chapter 6.

Computerized Psychological Testing

Although there is controversy over the current quality of computerized psychological testing (Fowler & Butcher, 1986; Matarazzo, 1983a, 1986), it is prevalent and on the increase. Although the ethical principle of assessment and the *Standards for Educational and Psychological Tests* (APA, 1985b) address issues related to computerized testing, they fall short of providing specific, practical guidelines for users. Therefore, the *Standards for the Administration and Interpretation of Computerized Psychological Testing* were developed (Hofer & Bersoff, 1983). A discussion of these standards follows.

The first section of the computer standards (Hofer & Bersoff, 1983) makes detailed recommendations about computer testing administration. These can be summarized as attempting to validate administration format; for instance, "Factors affecting test scores related to the computer presentation and recording of items that are irrelevant to the purposes of assessment should be eliminated" (Hofer & Bersoff, 1983, p. 30). Thus, one needs to be aware of the influence on results of computer hardware, test item display, understandability to the user, ability to change responses, and availability of a proctor. It is important to assure that the computer testing situation conforms to standardization guidelines, if available. Familiarity with research on conventional versus computerized testing, human factors, and ergonomics is certainly helpful.

So far as computerized psychological test scoring and interpretations go, there are two major concerns: (a) the adequacy of the scoring algorithms and the classification system used to assign statements to particular test scores, and (b) the validity of the interpretations inferred from test results (Hofer & Bersoff, 1983). *First,* the user should satisfy to herself or himself that the computer-generated scores (raw or scaled) are consistent with those derived by using traditional methods. Although computer hard copy looks accurate, such is not always the case, even after extensive field-testing by the company. *Second*, the user should have available data on the decision rules used to match test scores with interpretative statements. When this is not possible, the user should be aware of existing research on the computer programs being used. Unfortunately, this is often not available. *Third*, it is important to know which interpretive statements are linked to which test scores. Many computer-generated interpretations do not provide such information, making this guideline difficult to satisfy. Often one can scan the interpretative reports, comparing interpretations with test scores, to help assure validity. Once again, application to clinical health psychology requires use of appropriate norms in interpretation.

Fourth, it must always be kept in mind that computerized interpretive reports are *tools* of the qualified professional. The clinician is ultimately responsible for the report's validity and use (ethical principle of assessment). This means that the clinician might need to edit or amend the computer-generated psychological report, to take into account sound clinical judgment.

Clinical health psychologists are often involved in computerized psychological testing in the context of a medical center, a comprehensive treatment program (e.g. chronic pain program), or on an individual clinical treatment level. Matarazzo (1986) has voiced concern that "the tremendous advances during the past five years in microcomputerized psychological testing hardware and software have made it possible and economically seductive for a psychologist, a physician, another health service provider or a hospital administrator to offer such testing to unprecedented numbers of patients and clients" (p. 17).

Aside from being used by psychologists, computerized interpretive reports are being used by health care professionals, who are often accustomed to ordering lab tests from technicians. It would be easy for these reports to become just another piece of data, without interpretation by any psychologist familiar with the case. Yet most other health care professionals do not have specialized training in either psychological assessment or in specific ethical guidelines related to computerized psychological assessment to guide their behavior. It is difficult enough for psychologists, much less those untrained in psychometric assessment, to force themselves to scrutinize the slick computer report. The psychologist in these settings should watchdog how these systems are being used (or abused), assuming advocacy roles where appropriate.

SUGGESTED READINGS

American Psychological Association. (1981). *Ethical principles of psychologists.* Washington, DC: Author.

American Psychological Association. (1985). *Standards for providers of psychological services. (rev. 7th draft)*. Washington, DC: Author.

American Psychological Association. (1985). *Standards for educational and psychological testing*. Washington, DC: Author.

American Psychological Association. (1985). Ethics committee rules and procedures. *American Psychologist, 40*, 685–694.

Hofer, P. J., & Bersoff, D. N. (1983). *Standards for the administration and interpretation of computerized psychological testing*. Available from D. N. Bersoff, Suite 511, 1200 Seventeenth St. NW, Washington, DC 20036.

Keith-Spiegel, P., & Koocher, G. P. (1985). *Ethics in psychology*. New York: Random House.

Newman, A. S. (1981) Ethical issues in the supervision of psychotherapy. *Professional Psychology, 12* (6), 690–695.

Sales, B. D. (Ed.). (1983). *The professional psychologist's handbook*. New York: Plenum.

Chapter 5
Malpractice Risks in Clinical Health Psychology

Ideally, malpractice law serves three important social functions (Klein & Glover, 1983). *First*, it protects the public from professional wrongdoing by providing aversive consequences for misconduct. *Second*, it transfers the "loss" from one party to another who more evidently deserves to pay. *Third*, it distributes the cost of a professional's negligent action across the profession at large, through insurance premiums. In these ways, the threat of malpractice puts constant pressure on professional communities to self-regulate and self-scrutinize, while giving the public a mechanism to obtain recompense when this does not occur.

As evidenced by spiraling medical costs, partially related to increased malpractice litigation, it appears that the social function of malpractice law has been disrupted by consumers' propensity to initiate litigation. This may either occur when evidence of negligence can be found or, increasingly, when no negligence is ultimately determined. Skepticism about health care treatment and heightened anger over medical costs, combined with an increase in the number of attorneys per capita, has fostered the likelihood of malpractice litigation. Such legal actions are costly, even if the professional is exonerated. Often the case is settled out of court in an effort to avoid the higher expenditures, regardless of whether there was misconduct, thus reinforcing the tendency to file suits independent of the merits of the case. There is a societal cost for such freedom of action, which is ultimately passed back to consumers.

Mental health professionals have not been threatened by malpractice as much as physicians. This is thought to be due to the fact that the nature of the therapist–patient relationship inhibits such action and to the difficulty of proving the four malpractice standards to be described later. However, along with a greater public awareness of psychologists' professional behavior (Wright, 1981), malpractice claims in psychology are on the increase, a trend that is likely to continue. Although the APA's malpractice program had relatively few claims filed in the first 27 years of operation, 1955–1982 (Fisher, 1985; Wright, 1981), there has been a dramatic rise in claims since 1982. This increase in litigation against psychologists is reflected in a 700% rise in insurance premiums in the 2-year period from 1984 to 1986 (Fisher, 1985; Turkington, 1986).

Beyond public scrutiny of general psychological practice, psychologists working in the area of clinical health psychology open themselves to a myriad of new malpractice liability risks of which they should be aware (Knapp & Vandecreek, 1981). *First*, because clinical health psychologists practice in close concert with the medical profession and deal more often with physical problems, they run the risk of inadvertantly practicing medicine without a license. *Second*, the nature of the therapist–patient relationship, often thought to protect the traditional psychotherapy practitioner against malpractice, can be very different in many clinical health psychology cases. *Third*, physical harm is much more likely in the practice of clinical health psychology than in more traditional psychological treatment. This chapter will delineate general concepts of psychological malpractice and focus on those high-risk areas pertinent to clinical health psychology.

PSYCHOLOGICAL MALPRACTICE

Psychological Malpractice Defined

Malpractice is a professional error of commission or omission. Malpractice suits have generally been founded in tort or contract law, as opposed to criminal law. The difference is that the former pertains to acts offensive to an individual, whereas the latter applies to a transgression against society (Schutz, 1982). To make a successful malpractice case the plaintiff must prove, by a preponderance of evidence, the following four elements (Deardorff, Cross, & Hupprich, 1984; Feldman & Ward, 1979; Furrow, 1980; Harris, 1973): (a) the defendant-practitioner owed a "duty" to the patient; (b) the defendant-practitioner's behavior fell below the acceptable standard of care, or the "duty" owed to the plaintiff was otherwise breached; (c) the defendant-practitioner's act or omission was the proximate cause of the plaintiff's injury; and (d) an injury was actually sustained by the plaintiff. Each element is discussed next, with its implications for clinical health psychology.

Owing a duty to the patient. The first of these allegations, that the practitioner owed a duty to the patient, is usually the easiest to prove (Schutz,

1982). This basically involves proving that a professional relationship existed between the psychologist and the patient. Such things as a contract, a bill for services, or chart notes are sufficient evidence. Related to this contract, when a professional accepts a case, she or he has a duty to possess the level of skill to treat commensurate with that possessed by the average member of the profession in good standing in the community. Further, this skill and learning must be applied with reasonable care (Deardorff et al., 1984; *Professional Negligence*, 1973).

Proving a breach of duty. To prove a breach of duty, the plaintiff must show that the practitioner did not have the proper knowledge to treat or that this knowledge was misapplied. Outrageous actions such as beating a patient (*Hammer v. Rosen*, 1960) or engaging in sexual contact with a patient as part of treatment (*Roy v. Hartogs*, 1975) can provide a prima facia case of malpractice (Cross & Deardorff, 1987; Knapp, 1980). Other than in cases of this nature, proving a breach of duty has, historically, been difficult in an ambiguous practice such as psychotherapy. However, this might not be as true in the area of clinical health psychology. As discussed by Knapp and Vandecreek (1981), clinical health psychologists might have to adhere to more specifiable standards of care than traditional psychologists, as the techniques utilized can often be more explicitly delineated. Many treatments used in the practice of health psychology arise from behavioral, cognitive, and social learning frameworks with strong empirical bases; thus, aspects of treatment are often more measurable than in more psychodynamically oriented approaches. In the area of psychodiagnosis, techniques such as neuropsychological assessment are more open to validation and verification than more traditional projective techniques.

Generally, the standard of care against which the practitioner's behavior can be judged in malpractice litigation is established by expert testimony. In the past it has been difficult to get members of a profession to testify against one another (Markus, 1965), but this is less problematic since the courts abandoned the *locality rule*, which required the expert witness to be from the same geographical area as the defendant-practitioner. This change in court practice has had two important implications. *First*, it has successfully diminished the "conspiracy of silence" related to expert-witness testimony (Slovenko, 1979). *Second*, it means that a reasonable standard of care for psychological practice can be set at the national level instead of the community level, and the practitioner might have malpractice liability where state standards are below those of the national level (Pope, Simpson, & Myron, 1978). This could be especially relevant for the practice of clinical health psychology, as it is a relatively new and expanding area. Because there are likely to be fewer clinical health psychologists in a community, the court would be forced to draw expert witnesses from a more national geographical territory (Knapp & Vandecreek, 1981). Therefore, the standard of care could be set commensurate with a national, rather than a state, average minimum level of practice expertise. With this in mind, "Psychologists who expand their practices into this specialty should obtain appropriate training and expertise before presenting themselves to the public as specialists" (Knapp & Vandecreek, 1981, p. 680).

Proving proximate cause of patient's injury. The next allegation which must be proven is that the plaintiff's injury was directly caused by the practitioner's action or was a reasonably foreseeable consequence of such behavior. When the practitioner's behavior is not outrageous, proving this essential causal link between professional conduct and mental injury can be very difficult (Tarshis, 1972). However, if the injury is physical, proof is much easier (Dawidoff, 1966). In the practice of clinical health psychology, the injury is more likely to be physical, as the patient is often being treated for psychological factors affecting a physical condition. An example of this might be a psychologist's encouraging a cardiac patient to engage in an inappropriate amount of exercise without medical clearance, thus inducing a myocardial infarction.

Establishing an injury. The last element the plaintiff must demonstrate is that harm or injury was suffered. When physical harm has been sustained, it is easier to establish injury and specify monetary compensation; when the injury is emotional or psychological, it can be very difficult to establish compensation amounts (Klein & Glover, 1983). For instance, in the example of the cardiac patient, it would be relatively easier to estimate compensation based upon medical costs, physical disability, lost wages, and pain and suffering secondary to the physical damage than to estimate costs of emotional injuries.

AREAS OF MALPRACTICE RISK IN CLINICAL HEALTH PSYCHOLOGY

Practice of Medicine Without a License

One of the primary increased malpractice risks one encounters in moving from general clinical work to clinical health psychology involvement is that of practicing medicine without a license. Several authors have addressed this increased malpractice liability (Cohen, 1979; Furrow, 1980; Knapp & Vandecreek, 1981); their discussions are summarized below.

The practice of me_icine can be generally defined as "persons who diagnose or treat disease, or who represent themselves as healers of disease" (Knapp & Vandecreek, 1981, p. 678). Although the practice of medicine is clear in such things as surgery or chemotherapy, in other areas it becomes much less definable. These less clear areas relevant to "drugless healers" (e.g. psychologists) include diagnosing and treating patients within the bounds of one's own discipline and not crossing over into medical practice. Consider the following example:

> A. J. was a 37-year-old Black woman who presented with a complaint of headaches that had occurred daily over the past year. The headaches were characterized by a bandlike pain encircling the head. The pain began in the suboccipital region and radiated to posterior cervical areas. The patient reported no associated visual or gastrointestinal symptoms. The patient also stated that the headaches were exacerbated by stress, typically gaining in intensity over the course of the day. The patient had not had a recent physical exam. The psychologist performing the evaluation diagnosed the case as stress-related muscle contraction headaches and began treatment.

There are two problems with this case, from both liability and ethical standpoints. *First*, the patient had not had an appropriate medical workup related to the chief complaint. Within the practice of clinical health psychology, medical evaluation is almost always necessary. *Second*, the patient had not received a diagnosis of muscle-contraction headaches from a physician. Even though the symptom pattern is certainly suggestive of this disorder, from a legal viewpoint the psychologist could have been diagnosing a disease that would be considered within the realm of medical practice. This is because the "practitioner gave an opinion as to the origin or cause of the patient's physical ailments" (Knapp & Vandecreek, 1981, p. 678). However, it is perfectly appropriate for the health psychologist to make a diagnosis on Axis I of the DSM-III system (Diagnostic and Statistical Manual of Mental Disorders; American Psychiatric Association, 1980) such as "Psychological Factors Affecting Physical Condition" because the psychologist is not diagnosing the physical etiology of the problem.

Another problem is the legal implications of making a diagnosis on Axis III of the DSM-III. The nonphysician (or the psychiatrist who has not done a physical workup) must be careful not to give an Axis III diagnosis that he or she is either unqualified or unprepared to make. When recording an Axis III diagnosis, we find it most prudent to state where the physical diagnosis originated (for instance, "migraine headache per the patient," "per the medical record," "per the referral"). One must also take care in stating the source of the physical diagnosis in the text of the evaluation report. We have often seen statements that suggested the psychologist was making physical diagnoses.

Beyond diagnosing, clinical health psychologists must take care in treating physical disease. In the practice of clinical health psychology, the practitioner is often involved in the psychological or psychophysiological treatment of a physical problem. When the psychological treatment interferes with or takes the place of appropriate medical treatment, without informed consent, it is grounds for malpractice. There is a legal case history of nonphysician practitioners encouraging their patients to leave standard medical treatment and being held liable (see Cohen, 1979; Knapp & Vandecreek, 1981). Consider the following two examples:

B. J. was a 45-year-old, Caucasian male referred for adjunctive psycho-physiological treatment of his borderline hypertension (HTN). He was taking dyazide, which was controlling his HTN adequately, but he was excited about learning self-control techniques due to the aversive side effects of the medication. As the biofeedback and psychotherapy pro-gressed, B. J. was becoming increasingly able to decrease his blood pressure while relaxing in the clinic. He incessantly asked his therapist about reducing his medication with continued successful training. The psychol-ogist suggested this was an appropriate goal, and he was encouraged to carefully experiment with lower medication dosages while monitoring his HTN with a home monitoring unit.

The patient was an 82-year-old, Black female with congestive heart failure who was referred for treatment of a psycholophysiological disorder. The patient was on a complex medication regimen consisting of diuretics, potassium, and diazepam (Valium) prn (as needed) for anxiety and sleep. The patient was seen for an evaluation and then scheduled for a psycho-physiological baseline assessment. She was instructed not to take the Valium before the appointment, so that an accurate baseline assessment could be done. The patient came in the following week having not taken any of her medications for the day. Her legs were slightly edematous due to water retention. The patient had thought the clinical health psychologist prescribed that she not take any of her medications a day before the evaluation.

These two cases present clear examples of psychologists practicing medicine. This is not because reducing medications as the psychological techniques became more powerful was an inappropriate goal, but because these treatment directives must be done by the primary physician and be based on mutual consultation. Even more difficult decisions involve patients referred for treatment who are on prn medications. For example, we see many patients referred for psychophysiological treatment of their intractable chronic headaches who are on prn analgesic medication. Although there is no legal case history of whether a nonphysician health care practitioner can be held liable for problems resulting from encourag-ing a patient to reduce prn medications as treatment proceeds, the most prudent approach is to discuss this strategy with the physician and to document the results of this consultation.

Furthermore, the clinical health psychologist must be careful to insure that the patient does not mistake her or him for a physician. If this occurs, the practitioner could be held accountable for practicing medicine if a problem arises. In many medical centers, the likelihood of this occurring is increased by the dress code of the institution. Psychologists on both inpatient and outpatient services often wear traditional white lab coats. This can be confusing to patients, a confusion that can be readily ascertained by the nature of the patient's questions. In keeping with informed-consent procedures, on initial contact we make a concise statement about the psychologist's realm of expertise, which helps to avoid many problems in this area.

In general, based on case law involving other nonphysician health care professionals being sued for practicing medicine without a license, certain recommendations for practice are given: *First*, in providing psychological treatment for medical patients, one must work closely with the medical specialist. A joint treatment plan should be established. Further, this plan should be explicitly stated to the patient such that he or she understands which aspects of treatment will be handled by each professional. *Second*, when a self-referred patient seeks treatment for a problem involving a physical complaint, a medical evaluation should be insisted upon before treatment ensues. *Third*, one should communicate and consult, both verbally and in written form, with the primary physician on a periodic basis, so that both medical and psychological treatments can be jointly adjusted as appropriate. These consultations should be documented.

Duty to Prevent Patients from Harming Themselves

Whenever a suicidal patient presents to a mental health professional, action must be taken to prevent self-harm. When suicidal threats are not taken seriously or when an inadequate evaluation (judged by the community standard of care) is done, the practitioner can be liable in a malpractice action (Deardorff et al., 1984).

The suicidal patient can present a special risk for the clinical health psychologist working in a medical setting. More so than in traditional outpatient practice, clinical health psychologists evaluate suicidal patients in the emergency room and as medical inpatients. Thus, the evaluation and diagnosis of suicidality must be done rapidly and, typically, outside the context of a longer term treatment relationship. The clinical health psychologist must be familiar with the assessment of the suicidal patient and with appropriate precautionary measures (see Guggenheim, 1978, for review). When a therapist follows accepted evaluation and diagnostic procedures, and these do not reveal suicidality in a patient who subsequently commits suicide, there are no grounds for malpractice (*Baker v. United States*, 1964; see also Hogan, 1979, for a review of 38 cases involving suicidality).

As to addressing the process of managing the suicidal patient, Table 5.1 depicts several questions the clinician should ask herself or himself to guide the decision-making process (Bursztajn, Gutheil, Hamm, & Brodsky, 1983; Gutheil et al., 1983). The questions are consistent with sound clinical practice and are derived from legal standards of care against which professional behavior is judged. As can be seen in Table 5.1, these standards include: what a reasonable and prudent practitioner would do under similar circumstances, what the community standard of care is, and whether treatment benefits were maximized relative to possible costs or risks. The first two of these standards are essentially equivalent to the first two malpractice guidelines discussed earlier (that the practitioner owed a duty to the patient and that the practitioner's professional behavior fell below an acceptable standard of care). The last guideline is summarized by Cross and Deardorff (1987) in the following way:

> This is a cost benefit analysis in making treatment decisions. Related to the suicidal patient, the courts have not made it an ultimate goal that all suicides be prevented at any cost. Rather, the risks of certain treatment decisions (e.g., loosening the restraints on a suicidal patient or deciding to treat a suicidal patient on an outpatient basis) must be weighed against the therapeutic benefits to be gained (e.g., an increase in functioning). Thus, a practitioner does not have to be proved "right" by outcome, but rather that clinical judgment and decision-making fell within the three standards of care.

If a practitioner determines a patient to be suicidal, precautionary measures such as involuntary or voluntary commitment for observation might have to be invoked. If a patient is already in the hospital on a medical–surgical unit, other special issues arise. These include determining specific suicide precautions to be taken and making sure the staff carries them out.

Determination of the suicide precautions that must be taken is guided by a thorough assessment and evaluation of the patient. Table 5.2 depicts the suicide precautions that can be used on a medical–surgical unit, listed from most restrictive to least restrictive alternatives. Suicide precautions must be specified precisely in written form, either in the progress notes or in the doctor's orders section of the chart (depending on hospital guidelines). The psychologist must keep in mind that the staff is a nonpsychiatric one, and hence are generally not accustomed to implementing such procedures. The psychologist must also be prepared to deal with the staff's emotional response to the suicidal patient. On medical–surgical

Table 5.1. Questions derived from legal standards to facilitate management of suicidal patients

Reasonable and Prudent Practice

What is my implicit philosophy of science, the set of standards by which I judge my clinical reasoning to be "scientific"?

Am I focusing on a single cause of the patient's illness (or behavior) to the exclusion of other possible causes?

Am I being as sensitive as I can to the effects my own feelings might have on the assessment and treatment of this suicidal patient?

Did I adequately document my decision-making process?

Does the literature suggest methods of assessment and treatment that have been shown effective that I am not using?

Community Standards

Would anyone else take into account these same factors in making the treatment decision?

Would other clinicians feel as I do toward the patient? In other words, do my reactions tell me something about the way the patient affects others (especially those closest to him or her), rather than simply about myself?

Would one of my colleagues or, particularly, supervisors remind me of other considerations I am overlooking?

Maximization of Benefits Relative to Costs

Is this a situation where it is relatively safe to rely on the data I have?

Am I overlooking objective data, such as the statistical probability that someone with this patient's diagnosis would attempt suicide?

What if I am right about the consequences? Or what if I am wrong?

What will be the impact on the patient's immediate safety? On the patient's ultimate well-being? On the therapeutic alliance?

Am I sure enough of a high probability of small gains to risk a very low probability of a large loss?

Have I involved the patient as much as possible in the consideration of costs and benefits through the process of attempting to obtain informed consent? Are there any factors (costs or benefits) I am not considering?

Are there any data I have not considered (past medical or psychiatric records, significant others, staff input, patient input, etc.)?

Note. Adapted from "Subjective Data and Suicide Assessment in the Light of Recent Legal Developments," by H. Bursztajn, T. G. Gutheil, R. . Hamm, and A. Brodsky, 1981, International Journal of Law and Psychiatry, 6, p. 332.

Table 5.2. Examples of suicide precaution levels for use on an inpatient medical unit

Patient is in restraints (2- to 5-point) with a 24-hour "sitter" who observes constantly.

Patient is not restrained but has a 24-hour sitter who observes constantly, including toileting.

Patient has no sitter, but dangerous objects have been removed from the room including sharp objects, belts, combs, writing implements, glass objects, plastic bags (including wastebasket), and eating utensils. If patient is on medication, one might consider liquid to avoid "mouthing" or pill hoarding (especially where antidepressants are involved). There should be nursing checks every 15 to 30 minutes (or at some time interval). In setting check intervals, one should consider such things as whether patient has access to clothes and whether there are bars on the windows of the room. A suicide contract should be sought.

There are only nursing checks per unit standards, with no special suicide precautions. A suicide contract should be obtained that specifies that patient understands how to request help if suicidality increases.

units, where saving life is the primary goal, the staff often expresses anger and frustration toward a suicidal patient in indirect ways (such as not administering pain medications on time, or not speaking with the patient).

In making sure the staff carries out the suicide-precaution orders, the psychologist would be wise to initiate a staff intervention aimed at education and open communication about exactly what precautions are being taken, who is responsible for carrying them out, and what to do if problems arise. Of course, all information should be documented in the medical or nursing record. One must be particularly careful that adequate communication occurs across different nursing shifts. When this is done inadequately, negligent professional behavior could be found if litigation were to occur.

Duty to Protect

Increasingly, mental health professionals are being held responsible for protecting the public from violent acts of their patients. The duty to protect doctrine received great publicity in the case of *Tarasoff v. University of California* (1976), a case with which all mental health professionals should be familiar (see Kamenar, 1984). The court's ruling means that, although there might be no special relationship between a therapist and a victim, the relationship between a therapist and a patient is sufficient to impose special legal responsibility on the therapist for the patient's actions if the therapist knows the patient poses a serious threat or the therapist negligently fails to predict such dangerousness (Southard & Gross, 1983). The court's ruling also stated that, where danger to others exists, the confidential doctor–patient relationship must yield.

Since *Tarasoff* there has been much confusion in the mental health professions as to the specific implications of the ruling. Schindler (1976) noted that the courts offered no practical guidelines to follow. Southard and Gross (1983) and others (Beigler, 1984; Kamenar, 1984; Quinn, 1984; Wettstein, 1984) provided a thorough discussion of the misunderstanding surrounding the *Tarasoff* decision, while articulating the responsibilities of therapists related to the duty to protect.

Briefly, this case is often cited as "duty to warn," but the actual court decision was based on a "duty to care" or to protect. The courts did not rule that warning potential victims is a reasonable course of action in all cases; rather, the therapist is to take "reasonable care" to protect the potential victim (Knapp, 1980; Southard & Gross, 1983). Protective action involves many different possibilities.

Southard and Gross (1983) presented several cases that occurred after *Tarasoff* and that facilitate an understanding of the duty to protect doctrine. These findings include the facts that *Tarasoff* does not apply to suicide or to property damage (Schwitzgebel & Schwitzgebel, 1980), that it does not apply to nonspecific threats against nonspecific persons, and that imminence of danger is necessary for a duty to protect to exist. Based on these cases, Southard and Gross (1983) provided a "Tarasoff Decision Chart" (p. 41) to guide clinical decision making in executing a duty to protect (see Figure 5.1).

As can be seen in Figure 5.1, the initial steps (A, B) involve determining whether a "serious" threat exists. In these first two phases of assessment, a specific threat is not always the only criterion for invoking *Tarasoff*. If the professional "should have known" that a patient was dangerous to someone, as determined by standards of practice, then there was a *Tarasoff* responsibility (*McIntosh v. Milano* as cited in Kamenar, 1984). Step C deals with identifiability of the potential victim. Although there are no clear guidelines regarding identifiability, a discussion by Kamenar (1984) of several cases suggests that, even when the potential victim is not identifiable, the professional has a duty to "protect" a foreseeable but unidentifiable third party. This might include "detaining the patient, inquiring further as to the identity of the possible victim, warning his or her family or law enforcement officials, or taking some other precaution" (Kamenar, 1984, p. 265). Steps D through E involve determining whether danger is imminent and what group the intended victim might fall within. Throughout this process of decision making, documentation and consultation are of the utmost importance, because the clinician's actions will be judged by the reasonable and prudent practitioner guidelines and community standard of care. Steps F and G are possible actions, based upon assessment in the previous steps. Thus, warning the victim is not the sole possibility. In fact, some authors feel that the action taken by the

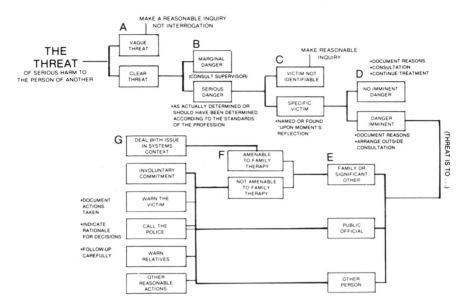

FIGURE 5.1. Tarasoff Decision Chart (*Note.* From "Making Clinical Decisions After Tarasoff" by M. J. Southard & B. H. Gross. In B. Gross & I. Weinberger (Eds.) *New directions for mental services. The mental health professional and the legal system, No. 16*, 1982, San Francisco: Jossey-Bass. Copyright 1982 by Jossey-Bass Publishers. Used with permission.)

therapists in the *Tarasoff* case was "rash" because, although threats were made, danger was not imminent, because Miss Tarasoff was out of the country. By having the patient who made threats against Tarasoff committed immediately, the therapists might have destroyed any therapeutic alliance that might have worked against the violent action that took place (Sadoff, 1979; Southard & Gross, 1983).

Although such decision-making trees are helpful, there is much concern that the courts are extending the duty to protect, related to the prediction of dangerousness, beyond what the scientific level of the profession is capable of delivering (Goodstein, 1985). A therapist's best defense is careful documentation, clinical reasoning, and consultation. Of course, these behaviors are all consistent with sound clinical practice.

The clinical health psychologist working in a hospital setting has a difficult task related to assessment and management of homicidality. He or she is most likely to be confronted with a *Tarasoff* situation while consulting to the emergency room or in the assessment of injured patients. Questions regarding perceived causation of the injury and possible motives for revenge are important. However, the health psychologist usually has not had a previous relationship with the patient; thus, adequate assessment is often difficult. In these situations, hospitalization may be utilized more frequently.

Confidentiality

Communication between patient and psychologist within the context of a professional relationship is considered confidential (APA, 1981). As with traditional psychological treatment, the clinical health psychologist is legally mandated to breach confidentiality under special circumstances (e.g. endangerment to others, child abuse, elder abuse, endangerment to self). When there is an inappropriate breach of confidentiality, it is grounds for malpractice (*Berry v. Moench*, 1958; *Furniss v. Fitchett*, 1958).

The practice of clinical health psychology can present special problems related to confidentiality (see chapters 4 and 8). One issue has to do with how much information related to the patient's psychological status, history, or condition is disclosed to the referral source, who is often the primary care physician with whom the clinician is probably working closely in the management of the patient.

Another issue involves the practice found in most medical centers in which patient files are relatively open for access to all professional staff. This, of course, presents problems for confidentiality of psychological services. Many departments of psychiatry and behavioral sciences maintain separate records, a policy that provides more control over access. One procedure we use for responding to a referral involves writing a detailed intake evaluation for our own records and then excerpting relevant parts to comprise a more general evaluation to be sent back to the referral source. In most cases this general report is also sent to the medical chart. The evaluation sent to the referral source is more symptom-focused and treatment plan-oriented. It does not include a detailed family history, particularly sensitive information, or a DSM-III diagnosis. Psychological material even of this general nature should be released only with the patient's knowledge. In many large health care systems, complete confidentiality cannot be promised, and the limits of confidentiality must be outlined to the patient in the informed-consent procedure.

Inpatient psychological treatment of medical patients presents problems with confidentiality similar to those just discussed among others. A major problem is how much information to document in the ward chart, which is perhaps more widely read than clinic charts. It is most prudent to follow the guidelines just presented in recording the most general and necessary information in the medical chart. It should be kept in mind that the psychological and behavioral information recorded in the ward chart can often affect how the staff interacts with the patient. When there is information particularly relevant to the treatment of the patient but not appropriate for the medical chart, the information should be verbally conveyed to the necessary health care professionals, and the fact that the patient's care was discussed should be documented in the medical chart.

Problems with confidentiality also occur when there is a release for medical information to an outside source, and psychological treatment progress notes or evaluations have been recorded in the medical chart (either inpatient or outpatient). General medical release-of-information forms are not sufficient to release psychological information, even when this information appears in the general medical record. This might seem obvious, but this issue is often overlooked in large medical systems. If the standard medical information release does not specify psychological information, it is important that the medical records department take appropriate precautions (such as blacking out psychological progress notes when copying medical records). It might ultimately be the psychologist's responsibility to be sure this is done.

Psychological Evaluation

Psychological evaluation is the area where psychologists are most likely to be sued for malpractice, and this pattern is likely to continue (Wright, 1981). The typical scenario is that the recommendation resulting from the psychological evaluation causes the patient/client to initiate a malpractice complaint concerning misuse of the test or test data. Wright concluded that in "most instances the filing of the grievance is a retaliatory expression of disappointment because something that the client wanted was denied or the client felt himself or herself to have been presented unfairly" (1981, p. 1490).

Clinical health psychologists, practicing within the limits of their specialty, would probably not be involved in those areas of psychological evaluation that have more frequently resulted in malpractice litigation. These include evaluations for employment decisions (hiring, firing, and promotion), child custody issues, and probation. However, clinical health psychologists are involved in psychological evaluations related to medical treatment or disability decision making (e.g., neuropsychological assessment; evaluation for inpatient pain programs; workmen's compensation assessments related to occupational injury; evaluation for penile prosthesis and other types of elective surgery) that could have increased malpractice risks. For instance, if a patient is denied access to a treatment program or surgery, or is given the opportunity for an alternative treatment that is more appropriate but not desired by the patient, a malpractice suit could be precipitated. In initiating the suit, the patient can deny the

validity of the findings and express disagreement with the recommendation. Consider the following case example:

> The patient was a 60-year-old married Caucasian male who was referred for
> psychological screening in conjunction with evaluation for a penile pros-
> thesis. For the past 5 years the patient had suffered from an erectile
> dysfunction that had precluded sexual intercourse. Medical evaluation had
> shown that blood flow and hormonal studies were within normal limits and
> that no physical etiology could be established. Nocturnal erections during
> sleep were intact. The patient was not informed about the implications of
> the psychological evaluation relative to his surgery, or about the feedback
> process, prior to being interviewed. The psychological evaluation revealed
> that there had been a number of significant marital problems at the time of
> the onset of the sexual dysfunction. In addition, the patient had been
> involved in an extramarital affair about which he felt very guilty. Recom-
> mendations included a course of behavioral sexual dysfunction therapy and
> marital counseling. The results of the evaluation were given to the surgeon,
> who subsequently met with the patient and gave him feedback as to the
> treatment decision. The patient stated adamantly that he was not interested
> in psychotherapy, that the problem was physically based, and that he
> wanted it resolved with the prosthesis. The patient brought a malpractice
> suit against the surgeon and the psychologist, stating he was denied the
> surgical procedure for unjustifiable reasons.

Of course, clinical health psychologists should not formulate recommendations following evaluations for the purpose of avoiding a malpractice suit. However, in the example just cited, the professionals made
several errors in handling informed consent that could have contributed
to the patient's ultimate legal action.

In general, the ways to minimize the risk of malpractice stem from what
would be considered sound clinical practice, regardless of the malpractice
issues. *First*, the patient should be fully informed about the nature of the
evaluation; for instance, who requested it, who will receive copies of the
results, where the results will be documented (psychiatric or medical
chart), ramifications of the results, and who will pay for it. After the
patient receives information on the evaluation process, some check of the
patient's understanding should be conducted and then a consent for the
evaluation obtained (see chapter 4). *Second*, after the evaluation, some
discussion of the findings should be held with the patient. This may occur
before or after consulting with the referring physician, depending on the
case, the psychologist's role as a consultant, and the relationship between
the psychologist and the physician. This feedback session with the
patient should include an opportunity for the patient to discuss her or his
reactions to the results and to ask any questions about processes or
procedures from then on. When there is a treatment team involved, it is
often advisable for the team or various members of the team (e.g. the
physician and the psychologist) to meet with the patient simultaneously

for feedback. In doing this, all questions that the patient might have can be addressed, reducing the risk of miscommunication or misinformation. *Fourth*, as suggested by Wright (1981), evaluation instruments should be given in the manner in which they were standardized, consistent with the standards for psychological testing. *Fifth*, careful documentation must be made of informed consent procedures, findings, the patient's response to the feedback session, consultation to the referral, and so forth.

Although the recommendations from psychological evaluations are not always consistent with patient desires, these guidelines can help reduce the risk of retaliatory or successful malpractice actions, without the practitioner's having to equivocate evaluation results to the point of uselessness.

Supervision of Trainees

The clinical health psychologist working in a supervisory capacity must be aware of increased malpractice liability. As the area of health psychology expands, increasing numbers of practitioners will be seeking supervision. In general clinical work, ethical issues related to supervision are just now beginning to be articulated (Newman, 1981). Certainly, one of the most important principles is that the clinical health psychology supervisor be competent to supervise in the specific area of practice. The following discussion assumes such competence.

Conceptually, the most important thing for the supervisor to bear in mind is that "the relationship of an assistant to a licensed professional is, legally, akin to an 'extension' of the professional himself" (Cohen, 1979, p. 237). However, both parties must understand that the trainee should not function in such a manner that the public would be led to believe that he or she is a fully licensed professional or expert in the field if that is not the case.

Another point is that the amount of supervision must be based on the needs of the supervisee and the patient (Cohen, 1979). Setting up a structured schedule of supervision is reasonable, and commonly practiced, but it should be flexible enough to accommodate clinical issues or problems as they arise.

Related to schedules of supervision, a record of the supervisory activity should be kept. This is most easily done in the patient's chart and need not be done at every supervisory session. Rather, the supervisor should periodically document that there is agreement with the supervisee's diagnostic formulation and treatment plan. This guideline should also be followed if the trainee is doing inpatient work and charting in the medical record. In fact, many medical facilities require the supervisor to countersign all charted information.

These recommendations afford increased legal protection for the supervisee and the supervisor. Although the supervisory relationship creates supervisor liability for the professional behavior of her or his trainees, the supervisee is not totally absolved of responsibility in malpractice action. Thus, documenting supervision times and following the previously suggested guidelines offer protection of both parties and provide for higher quality supervision.

SUMMARY AND CONCLUSIONS

This chapter has outlined general concepts of malpractice law, and it has delineated several areas of increased malpractice risk particularly relevant to the practice of clinical health psychology. We have attempted to provide concrete examples of the more common dilemmas that occur in clinical health psychology practice. Even so, the clinical health psychology practitioner may frequently be faced with unique ethical and legal problems. As clinical health psychology is a relatively young area, consultation with one's colleagues, ethical panels, and legal counsel is advisable when faced with professional practice issues.

SUGGESTED READINGS

Cohen, R. J. (1979). *Malpractice: A guide for mental health professionals.* New York: Free Press.

Deardorff, W. W., Cross, H. J., & Hupprich, W. R. (1984). Malpractice liability in psychotherapy: Client and practitioner perspectives. *Professional Psychology: Research and Practice, 15,* 590–600.

Furrow, B. (1980). *Malpractice in psychotherapy.* Lexington, MA: D. C. Heath.

Gable, R. K. (1983). Malpractice liability of psychologists. In B. D. Sales (Ed.) *The professional psychologists' handbook.* New York: Plenum.

Knapp, S. (1980). A primer on malpractice for psychologists. *Professional Psychology, 11,* 606–612.

Knapp, S., & Vandecreek, L. (1981). Behavioral medicine: Its malpractice risks for psychologists. *Professional Psychology, 12,* 677–683.

Schutz, B. M. (1982). *Legal liability in psychotherapy: A practitioner's guide to risk management.* San Francisco: Jossey-Bass.

Chapter 6
Clinical Health Psychology Assessment

As indicated in chapter 1, although precise data are not available, psychodiagnostic assessment is one of the most frequent activities of clinical health psychologists. It is also probably one of psychology's most unique contributions to patient care. Although assessment is often used by the psychologist as the first step in developing a treatment program for his or her own patient, in clinical health psychology it is frequently used to answer questions and thus solve problems regarding patient care for another health professional. As Osler, the well-known physician, so aptly stated, "It is more important to know what kind of man has a disease than to know what kind of disease a man has" (Osler, 1971, p. 14). For clinical health psychologists, the assessment activity is, then, inextricably intertwined with the consultation activity.

The kinds of consultation requests made of clinical health psychologists partially depend, of course, upon the kind of practice one has delineated. Additionally, the kinds of referral bases developed (e.g., pediatric, neuropsychological) influence the types of assessment questions posed. We do not know of any published data on the kinds of referrals made to a single-discipline clinical health psychology service, but there are reports available about referral patterns to multidisciplinary consultation–liaison psychiatry teams. Lipowski (1967) described the kinds of diagnostic issues that the consultant is likely to encounter.

1. Psychological presentations of organic disease (e.g., pancreatic cancer presenting as depression)
2. Psychological complications of organic disease (e.g., postcardiotomy delirium)
3. Psychological reactions to organic disease (e.g., depression subsequent to amputation)

4. Somatic effects of psychological distress (e.g., angina)
5. Somatic presentations of psychiatric disorder (e.g., masked depression)

A report by Shevitz, Silberfarb, and Lipowski (1976) on 1,000 referrals for psychiatric consultation in a general hospital found that approximately 57% of the patients were referred for differential diagnosis, 56% were referred for management problems (disturbing behavior on the ward, psychiatric disorders that complicated a known organic disease, and somatic problems with no known organic pathology), and 28% were referred for disposition, especially after a suicide attempt that mandated a psychiatric referral.

From the senior author's experience directing the medical psychology service at a major academic medical center, it seems that a wide variety of medical–surgical patients are likely to be referred specifically to clinical health psychologists. Although it appeared that the psychiatric services at the same center tended to receive the consultations concerning suicidal and combative behavior, psychotropic medication, and mental status changes, the psychologists received relatively more consultation requests concerning such issues as coping with illness, compliance, preparation for surgery, presurgical screenings, diagnostic and treatment issues associated with chronic pain, and, of course, neuropsychological evaluations.

We have more recent data from our experience in developing a behavioral medicine outpatient team in an HMO setting. During the first 6 months of its functioning, we received over 250 referrals. Although nearly half of those involved requests from neurology, internal medicine, and family practice units to provide services in the areas of headache management and neuropsychological assessment, a significant number of other clinical problems were seen for consultation or treatment purposes. These included such varied disorders as tinnitus, Raynaud's phenomenon, irritable bowel syndrome, angina, compliance issues following myocardial infarction, temporomandibular joint pain, penile prosthesis surgery, blepharospasm, chronic vomiting, neurodermatitis, fibrositis, and hypertension.

In general, we believe that the growth of the applied research base within health psychology has resulted in an increased need for clinical services in areas not always addressed by traditional consultation and liaison psychiatry or clinical psychology models. Specifically, these include:

1. Consultations and treatments involving psychophysiologic self-regulation or the application of learning theory, either as the treatment of choice for a medical problem or as an adjunct to standard medical care

2. Consultations involving psychometric predictions of response to medical–surgical treatments
3. Reduction of health-risk behaviors.

Given the possible range of consultation and assessment activities in clinical health psychology, it will not be possible to detail problems associated with specific diseases or to address the utility of specific assessment measures that are well described elsewhere (Karoly, 1985; Keefe & Blumenthal, 1982; Prokop & Bradley, 1981). Instead, we shall focus on a *model* for assessment in clinical health psychology and then focus on *process-oriented issues* that are common among various settings, roles, and types of illnesses. Special attention will be paid to the attendant difficulties for the clinical health psychologist in completing a psychological assessment.

A MODEL FOR ASSESSMENT IN CLINICAL HEALTH PSYCHOLOGY

Following the medical model, psychological assessment has traditionally had two primary purposes: identification and treatment of psychological disorders. As such, psychological assessment measures have been developed to focus on a single dimension of the patient—namely, the state of the patient's mind—without complementary consideration of the patient's body. Conversely, medicine has traditionally focused on the treatment of disease to the exclusion of personality or emotional factors. Each approach has some value, but the field of clinical health psychology requires integration of these divergent attitudes (often in the absence of adequate conceptual models); adequate assessment cannot afford to exclude one for the other.

The clinical health psychologist's tasks are to assess the interactions among the person, the disease, and the person's environment and to formulate a diagnostic or treatment strategy based on that understanding. Given the necessity of incorporating physiological, psychological, and sociological information, the clinical health psychologist typically works from a biopsychosocial perspective of health and illness (Engel, 1977). Based on Engel's work and that of Leigh and Reiser (1980), we have elaborated a model for assessment that we find useful in approaching clinical situations because it facilitates organization of information and subsequent decision-making about assessment strategies. Unfortunately, this model reduces various aspects of the biopsychosocial perspective in a manner that could enhance thinking in a compartmentalized, reductionistic fashion about complex interrelated processes. The reader is reminded that this is not reflective of our overall orientation toward assessment issues but is, rather, an artifact of inadequacies in current schemata representing the biopsychosocial model.

TARGETS OF ASSESSMENT

Table 6.1 conveys the targets of assessment by nature of information (biological or physical, affective, cognitive, behavioral) and unit of assessment (patient, family, health care system, sociocultural context). Within each block are listed examples of the kinds of information that need to be gathered when conducting the assessment or of which the clinician should be aware when attempting to understand the patient from a biopsychosocial perspective. Each block also has an associated developmental or historical perspective, which could be critical to an understanding of the present condition and to the prediction of the future course of action. In each area, the clinician should attempt to understand the patient's current status, changes since onset of the illness, and past history. The focus of the assessment should not be solely on identification of problems but also on delineation of assets, resources, and strengths of the patient and his or her environment.

Patient Targets

Biological targets. The most obvious biological targets are the patient's age, race, sex, and physical appearance. In addition, the clinician needs to gain a thorough understanding of the patient's current physiological symptoms and how they are similar or different from past symptoms. Recent physical changes could be particularly salient to the assessment, as they are often the precipitating events that elicit the referral (e.g., recent hair loss due to radiation treatment, incontinence, gross pedal edema following noncompliance with dietary regimen). The clinician will want to obtain information on the specifics of the particular disease including nature, location, and frequency of symptoms; current treatment regimen; and health status within the disease process (e.g., Stages I through IV in cancer). Other sources of biological information include the physical exam, current and past vital signs, the results from relevant laboratory tests (e.g., creatinine levels, blood alcohol levels, white blood counts), medications, and use of illicit drugs. Further, a history of the patient's constitution and general health, including previous illnesses, relevant genetic information, injuries, and surgeries, should be obtained.

Depending upon the problem, biological targets might also include variables associated with the autonomic nervous system or musculo-skeletal activity (e.g., electromyographic [EMG] recordings, peripheral temperature readings) obtained in both resting and stress-related conditions. For example, a psychophysiological profile involving frontal EMG activity might be obtained on a patient suffering from tension headache.

Affective targets. The assessment of affective targets includes understanding the patient's current mood and affect, their contextual elements and historical features. In addition, in clinical health psychology, an assessment would be incomplete without having obtained information about the patient's *feelings* about his or her illness, treatment, health care providers, future, social support network and, of course, self.

Again, it is helpful to obtain data that allow for comparison between current affective states and those of the past in that it is often the contrast that has prompted the referral. For example, a request we received stated, "Patient recently diagnosed with colon cancer. Had been adjusting well to pending surgery, now crying frequently. Please evaluate." It was the *change* in affective state that led to this referral, a change that turned out to be related to a family problem rather than difficulty in coping with illness. Previous history of affective disturbance must also be obtained.

Cognitive targets. Assessment of the patient's cognitive functioning involves gathering information about the patient's knowledge, perceptions, and attitudes, as well as content and pattern of thinking. It is imperative that the clinical health psychologist be aware of cognitive abilities and limitations of the patient, from both current and developmental perspectives. Cognitive targets include general intelligence; educational level; specific knowledge concerning illness and treatment; attitudes toward health, illness, and health care providers; perceived threat of illness; perceived control over psychological and physical symptoms; perception of costs and benefits of possible treatment regimens; and expectations about future outcome. Another important target is the perceived *meaning* of the illness to the patient. More generally, the clinician should be aware of the patient's general cognitive style and philosophy of life, including religious beliefs.

Behavioral targets. Behavioral targets include what the patient is doing (the action) and the manner in which he or she does it (the style). Action primarily involves assessment of motoric behaviors such as facial expressions, foot tapping, bruxing, bracing, body posture, and eye contact. Styles are varied but include flamboyant, hesitant, age-appropriate, hostile, restless, passive, and cooperative. The clinical health psychologist will want to understand the patient's overall level, pattern, and style of activity in areas of self-care and interpersonal, occupational, and

Table 6.1. Targets of assessment

Nature of information	Patient	Environment		
		Health care system	Family	Sociocultural context
Biological or Physical	Age, sex, race Physical appearance Symptoms, health status Physical exam Vital signs, lab data Medications, drugs Psychophysiological data Constitutional factors Genetics History of injury, disease, and surgery	Characteristics of the treatment setting Characteristics of medical procedures and treatment regimens Availability of prosthetic aids	Characteristics of the home setting Economic resources Size of family Familial patterning (history of headache) Other illness in family members	Social services Financial resources Social networks Occupational setting Physical job requirements Health hazards
Affective	Mood Affect Feelings about illness, treatment, health care, providers, self, family, job, and social network History of affective disturbance	Providers' feelings about patient, illness, and treatment	Members' feelings about patient, illness, and treatment	Sentiment of culture regarding patient, illness, and treatment

Cognitive	Cognitive style Thought content Intelligence Education Knowledge about disease Health beliefs Attitudes and expectations regarding illness, treatment, health care, and providers Perceived meaning of illness Philosophy of life	Providers' knowledge Providers' attitudes toward patient, illness, and treatment	Knowledge about illness and treatment Attitudes and expectations about patient, illness, and treatment Intellectual resources	Current state of knowledge Cultural attitudes toward patient and illness
Behavioral	Activity level Interactions with family, friends, providers, and co-workers Health habits Health care utilization (previous medications and psychological treatment) Compliance Ability to control physical symptoms	Providers' skills in educating and training patients Reinforcement contingencies for health and illness	Participation in patient care Reinforcement contingencies for health and illness	Employment policies Laws regulating health care practice, disability, provision of care, health habits Handicapped access Customs in symptom reporting and help seeking

recreational functioning, as well as specific behavioral targets related to the reason for referral. Of special interest is the patterning and nature of the doctor–patient relationship, as well as whether the patient can voluntarily control any of her or his physical symptoms. Once again, a historical perspective is important, as past behavior is often the best predictor of future behavior.

Extremely important in clinical health psychology is the assessment of current and previous health habits (e.g., smoking, exercise, eating patterns) and health care utilization. The clinician should be able to answer the following questions about the patient: What are the nature, frequency, and pattern of past contacts with health service providers? What have been the antecedent stimuli and consequences of these contacts (i.e., history of previous help seeking and treatments)? Finally, an assessment would be incomplete without information concerning the patient's current and past history of compliance or adherence to treatment regimens, with specific reasons noted for noncompliance whenever it has occurred. Areas of assessment here include medication usage as prescribed, history of keeping appointments, and follow-through on previous recommendations.

Environmental Targets

The clinical health psychologist also needs to assess aspects of the various environments within which the patient interacts: (a) the family unit, (b) the health care system with its various settings and providers, and (c) the sociocultural environment including social network, cultural background features, and occupational setting. As with assessment of the individual patient, targets of assessment include physical, affective, cognitive, and behavioral components of these environments, stressing the demands, limitations, and supports that these aspects of environments entail.

Family environment. In assessing the physical domain of the family environment, it is important to know about available economic resources and perhaps even physical characteristics of the home setting, depending upon the problem being assessed (e.g., quadriplegia). The family's developmental history, size, and experience of recent changes are all important aspects to consider. The clinician should also be aware of other illnesses in family members (e.g., history of hypertension, diabetes) and familial patterning of symptoms (e.g., headaches).

In the affective realm, it is important to understand family members' feelings about the patient, his or her illness, and the treatments rendered. Assessment of past or present affective disturbance in the family is essential. In the cognitive arena, the clinician must assess the family's attitudes, perceptions, and expectations about the patient, her or his illness and treatment, and the future. Family members' intellectual resources, as well as knowledge they possess about health and illness, should also be understood.

In the behavioral realm, the clinician will want to know whether there have been any changes within the family since the onset of the illness, such as a shift in roles and responsibilities of family members, and to find out to what degree family members participate in the patient's care. Assessment of behaviors of family members that could influence the patient's illness or adaptation is crucial. For example, families may model chronic illness, punish self-help attempts and be secretive in a manner that increases patient anxiety.

Health care system. The health care system should also be assessed across physical, affective, cognitive, and behavioral domains. For example, in the first domain, the clinician needs to know the physical characteristics of the setting in which the patient is being assessed or treated e.g., anxiety, coronary care unit, ward, outpatient clinic). Special considerations include degree of sensory stimulation, privacy, and availability of prosthetic aids. The clinical health psychologist must understand the physical characteristics of the diagnostic procedures and the treatment regimen to which the patient has been, is being, or will be exposed (e.g., pelvic exenteration, colostomy, hemodialysis, chemotherapy). The costs, side effects, and benefits of each of these procedures, as perceived by the patient, should also be assessed.

In the affective realm, one must be aware of how health care providers feel about the patient and about the patient's illness (e.g., requests for sterilization). Special problems can occur, for example, in burn units, where both perpetrators and victims of severely injurious events can be housed within the same unit. Staff and visitors often feel split in their feelings and loyalties to these patients. Also, the attitude of specific providers toward the health care system within which they work can enhance or detract from overall health care.

In the cognitive domain, the clinician needs to understand how knowledgeable health care providers are about the patient's problems, illness, and treatment, and needs to assess their attitudes and expectations about these matters as well as the patient's future.

When assessing the behavior of the overall health care system, the clinician needs to be aware of policies, rules, and regulations that will affect the patient and his or her treatment (for example, staffing patterns, single or rotating physicians, appointment schedules, infection-control policies). It is important to understand what specific behaviors health care providers might display that could influence patient behavior (such behaviors might include transmitting knowledge about disease, providing skill training in self-care, reinforcing verbal complaints, or avoiding affective expression by the patient).

Sociocultural environment. Physical aspects of the patient's sociocultural environment include both (a) the physical requirements and flexibilities of the patient's occupation and work setting and (b) the social and financial resources and services available to the patient. In addition, the clinician should be aware of the nature of the patient's social network including size, density, and proximity and the frequency of the patient's contact with it. Assessment of the natural environment in terms of ecological health hazards (e.g., pollutants) is also sometimes necessary.

In the affective realm, the clinician should understand cultural sentiments about the patient's race, ethnicity, life-style, and illness (e.g., "AIDS hysteria"). It is also advantageous to be aware of the current state of knowledge or community standard of care for the patient's problem.

In assessing cognitive features, one needs to know relevant cultural attitudes and expectations regarding the patient, the illness, and the treatment. Questions that come to mind include What are the cultural attitudes toward prevention? In general, what is the health-belief model of the culture?

In terms of the behavior of large sociocultural systems, the clinician might need to know specific employment policies related to the problem being assessed (e.g., regulations regarding return to work for patients with back pain, hiring guidelines for AIDS patients). In addition, certain legislation regulating health care provision and health habits might be relevant (e.g., disability payments, diagnostic related groups [DRGs], smoking in public places). Finally, the clinician should be aware of ethnic customs that could be related to symptom reporting (or underreporting) and health care utilization.

INTEGRATING BASIC
ASSESSMENT INFORMATION

It becomes clear from a review of these assessment targets and the information to be obtained under each heading that these "blocks" are interrelated and that the nature or relative importance of information obtained under one heading is often affected by information found in another block. For example, type and location of physical symptoms can affect perceived meaning of the illness because of the special psychological significance of certain bodily parts (e.g., genitalia, heart). Thus affective reactions could be more pronounced in a patient with cervical carcinoma *in situ* than those found in an individual with an objectively worse health status (e.g., insulin-dependent diabetes). However, this affective reaction can also be mediated by age, because the loss of ability to bear children can be significantly less traumatic for a 55-year-old woman than for a 17-year-old teenager. Cultural attitudes can attenuate this relationship even further. For example, in rural Florida, black females undergoing hysterectomy were considered "no longer women"; this cultural attitude affected not only their emotional reactions but also their health care utilization. We are also aware of more cavalier attitudes on the part of a few physicians about conducting hysterectomies when the potential recipients were unwed females, of low socioeconomic status, with multiple children. These attitudes can effect not only clinical decision-making, and thus treatments rendered, but also the characteristics of the health care environment and the doctor–patient relationship.

In conducting an assessment, it is important to understand that the data obtained can be influenced by the type of setting in which the assessment is occurring. For example, patients with low back pain often walk with greater or lesser flexibility depending on who is watching them and in what setting they are being observed. The authors are reminded of the following example: A low back pain patient in an inpatient chronic pain program was repeatedly observed ambulating with a walker by program personnel. On one occasion, though, when the patient was unaware he was being observed, he was seen casually carrying his walker over his shoulder while ambulating with appropriate body posture and gait. We also know that there are physiological effects of various social environments. Examples of this phenomenon include synchronization of menstrual cycles in college women living together, light–dark cycles as synchronizers of various biological rhythms, and synchronized cycles of heart rates of children in play groups (see Warner, 1982, for review).

Settings also have different base rates of certain phenomena. For example, there appear to be more risk takers on orthopedic wards (which tend to have more accident victims such as motorcycle riders), and it has been shown that, in general, patients in teaching hospitals report more anxiety than patients in community hospitals (Lucente & Fleck, 1972). The presence of other people, their roles and behavior can also effect responses during assessment. We have more than once witnessed the emotional breakdown of a patient only a few minutes after the patient assured the oncologist that she or he was "doing well." The breakdown was not observed until the oncologist left the room, in part due to the need to be a "good patient" for the physician, who is perceived as having so much power over life and death. We have also experienced the reluctance of patients to reveal even significant physical symptoms because they perceived their physicians as being "too rushed." These types of interrelationships are obviously complex. We are reminded of the case of the 75-year-old male who, in a late stage of chronic obstructive pulmonary disease, manifested his anxiety by "grumbling at staff." Staff consequently avoided him, thus reinforcing his fear of dying alone and his complaints of poor care.

Relationships among the building blocks of assessment that influence the interpretation of obtained information include the effects of:

1. Medication on psychophysiological recordings (e.g., diazepam on EMG level)
2. Fund of knowledge of the physician, or on medical diagnosis (often specialists need to be consulted to evaluate medical record data, as the referral might have come from a general practitioner who had not completely evaluated the presenting problem)
3. Family understanding and involvement in treatment on compliance with medical regimen
4. Family reactions on self-care activities (e.g., overprotectiveness often impedes patient self-management and, consequently, hinders development of a sense of mastery)
5. Legislation on sick-role behavior (e.g., disability payments could reinforce chronic illness behavior)
6. Religious beliefs on the perceived meaning of symptoms and acceptance of medical regimens (e.g., pain as guilt for past sins, refusal of a therapeutic abortion for a life-threatening pregnancy)
7. Providers' attitudes about disease on patients' affective responses (e.g., nurses' refusal to minister to AIDS patients)
8. Family attitudes toward disease on patients' affective and behavioral responses (e.g., wife's negative attitude about colostomy contributing to patient's impotence)
9. Prosthetic characteristics of environment on patient activity level (e.g., a barrier-free environment facilitates activity level for the spinal cord patient)
10. Occupational requirements on self-esteem (e.g., loss of breadwinning capacity by artist who loses functioning in dominant hand)
11. Providers' attitudes toward treatments on patient suffering (e.g., negative attitudes about use of narcotics resulting in undermedication of cancer pain)
12. Cognitive factors on course of illness (e.g., maintenance of hope and future orientation facilitating recovery from surgery; unrealistically positive expectations about sexual functioning associated with poor outcome in penile prosthesis surgery)
13. Cognitive factors on physical symptoms (e.g., perceived control of pain results in increased tolerance for pain)

This sample demonstrates the multitude of interactions that might occur among various targets of assessment. Obviously, to be able to competently interpret data obtained, one needs a firm grounding in the theoretical and empirical health psychology literature listed in the suggested readings sections found at the ends of most chapters of this book. In developing a conceptualization of the case, the clinician differentially weights information based on mediating relationships as demonstrated via research and as learned through his or her experience in working with patients. There is no substitute for good clinical judgment.

METHODS OF ASSESSMENT

In performing the clinical health psychology assessment, there are numerous methods that may be utilized. Many of these will give information about one or more targets in our assessment model. Choice of method depends upon the target being assessed, the purpose of the assessment, and the skill of the clinician. We are not wedded to any one particular technique, as each has its strengths and weaknesses, although we rely heavily upon a good clinical interview as a core clinical method. We endorse a multiple-measurement model and a convergent, hypothesis-testing approach to clinical assessment. Detailed descriptions of specific methods will not be provided, but we shall list the core techniques utilized in clinical health psychology. There are currently two excellent references for further study in this area: Karoly (1985) and Keefe and Blumenthal (1982). We shall discuss the following methods of assessment: interview, questionnaires, diaries, psychometrics, observation, psychophysiological measures, and archival data.

Interview

The clinical interview is perhaps the most common method of gathering information. It has the capacity to elicit current and historical data across all target areas: physical, affective, cognitive, and behavioral targets for the patient and for her or his family, health care, and sociocultural environments. The interview is also a means of developing a supportive working relationship with the patient. It permits the acquisition of self-report and observational data from the patient, family members, significant others, employers, and health care providers. Understanding one's own stimulus value is crucial to the interpretation of interview data.

Content and style of individual interviews vary, depending upon the assessment question. The formality of the interview process (unstructured, semistructured, or structured) often depends on the personal preference of the clinician, as well as the setting and time constraints. Specific intervention programs (e.g., presurgical penile prosthesis screenings, headache treatment programs) commonly use structured interviews, but we prefer a combination of structured and unstructured approaches in an effort to avoid interviewer bias and to remain open to exploring target areas not immediately recognized as important.

One structured interview that has received a good deal of attention in the health psychology literature is the Type A Structured Interview (Rosenman, 1978). Although its development could serve as a model for other such assessment techniques, it tends to be used more for research than for clinical purposes. (A thorough review of the Type A area can be found in Matthews, 1982.) Also of special interest is the Psychosocial Adjustment to Illness Scale (PAIS) described by Derogatis (1986). There are both structured interviews and self-report (PAIS-SR) formats, designed to assess domains of health care orientation, vocational environment, sexual relationships, extended family relationships, social environment, and psychological distress.

There are some instances in which patient interviews are impossible. Occasionaly the patient is too agitated or not sufficiently alert to meet the demands of the interview. There are also times in which the patient is uncooperative, in which case the clinician needs to use alternative forms of assessment, delay the consultation, or discontinue the process in the absence of adequate consent.

Questionnaires

Clinician developed, problem-focused, information-gathering questionnaires can be very useful in the assessment process. In the outpatient setting, these can be mailed to patients prior to the first visit and reviewed at the time of interview. We have found this method to be a considerable time-saver in the evaluation of chronic pain patients. The interviewer may review questionnaire data with the patient but can focus more time on areas needing further clarification and on more general psychological issues. Reviewing some data with the patient is also important to demonstrate the value of the data to the clinician, which could affect future patient compliance. Questionnaires are also a mechanism for the systematic recording of data that can facilitate later clinical research and program evaluation.

Our intake questionnaire for use with chronic-pain patients consists of some 80 questions related to the presenting problem, previous treatments, and effects on daily functioning. In the hundreds of patients who have been asked to complete various versions of this questionnaire, refusal has been almost nonexistent. However, given the initial defensiveness of many patients to seeing a psychologist, we have found it important to limit questionnaire items to variables related to sociodemographic features and the chief complaint, leaving more psychologically oriented exploration to the interview.

Questionnaires can also be developed for significant others and health care providers. The form and content of the questionnaire will depend, of course, on the theoretical orientation of the clinician. Questions may be forced-choice, open-ended, simple rating, checklist, or pictorial in nature (e.g., pain maps). Clarity and ease of response are important features. However, the clinician must take care not to use questionnaire techniques in a fashion that would substitute for the development of a quality professional relationship with either the patient or the referral source.

Diaries

Patient diaries are commonly used to record both overt (e.g., vomiting, tics, activity level, frequency of urination, medication usage) and covert (e.g., thoughts, feelings, images, blood pressure, body temperature) behaviors. They are used as baseline measures and as a treatment technique to foster learning (both psychological and physiological insights) about antecedents, consequences, and relationships among internal and external behaviors. Diaries are also used to measure the effectiveness of treatment programs. There are controversies about the reliability and validity of diary data, but these methods continue to be clinically useful.

Diaries should be easy to use, brief, and nonintrusive. Training the recorder in their use is important. The use of cues as reminders to record or mail in forms can increase compliance. It should be noted that not all diaries are maintained by the patient. Medical charting and psychiatric process notes are two examples of diaries that are maintained by staff.

Psychometrics

In general, there are two kinds of psychometric techniques used in clinical health psychology: broadband and narrow-focus measures. Listed next are some of the most frequently used measures with which the clinician should be familiar. However, one should be cautious in the application of these measures to clinical health psychology, carefully evaluating their suitability for medical–surgical or dental patient populations and for the specific problems being addressed. Broadband measures include:

1. *The Minnesota Multiphasic Personality Inventory* (MMPI; Hathaway & McKinley, 1967). Perhaps the most commonly used measure in clinical

health psychology, the MMPI was designed as a measure of psychopathology, and appropriate norms must be used when interpreting
results for medical–surgical populations.

2. *The 16 Personality Factor Inventory* (16PF; Cattell, Eber, & Tatsouka,
   1970). Developed as a measure of personality, this test might be more
   appropriate to medical–surgical populations than the MMPI when the
   focus is not assessment of psychopathology.

3. *Projective techniques* such as the Rorschach (Rorschach, 1942) and the
   Thematic Apperception Test (Murray, 1938). These techniques of
   personality assessment require considerable time to administer and to
   interpret, and the constructs measured frequently cannot be translated
   into overt behavior.

5. *Millon Behavioral Health Inventory* (MBHI; Millon, Green, & Meagher,
   1982b). This test was designed specifically with medical–behavioral
   decision-making in mind. It attempts to assess not only basic coping
   styles but also feelings and perceptions of the individual that are
   thought to aggravate the course of current disease or increase suscepti-
   bility to disease.

There are also a number of more narrowly focused instruments used in
the practice of clinical health psychology. A subgroup of these measure
general psychological constructs, experiences, or symptoms:

1. *Beck Depression Inventory* (BDI; Beck, 1972). A measure of severity of
   depression.

2. *State-Trait Anxiety Inventory* (STAI; Spielberger, Gorsuch, & Lushene,
   1979). A self-report measure of anxiety.

3. *Symptom Check List-90* (SCL-90; Derogatis, 1977). A checklist of psychiatric symptomatology.

4. *Index of Activities of Daily Living* (ADL; Katz, Downs, Cash, & Grotz,
   1970). A measure of independent functioning most useful for geriatric
   and institutionalized populations.

5. *Measures of life events* such as the Schedule of Recent Experience (SRE;
   Holmes & Rahe, 1967) and the Life Experiences Survey (LES; Sarason,
   Johnson, & Siegel, 1978), the latter of which includes an assessment
   of the perceived significance of the event.

6. *Cognitive Capacity Screening Exam* (CCSE; J. Jacobs, Bernhard,
   Delgado, & Strain, 1977). A brief, scorable, mental status questionnaire that is easily administered as a screening device.

7. *Mini-Mental-State* examination (Folstein, Folstein, & McHugh, 1975).
   A method of grading the cognitive state of patients.

8. *Family Environment Scale* (FES; Moos & Moos, 1981). An assessment of
   three domains of family environment; (a) quality of interpersonal
   relationships, (b) personal growth goals, and (c) system maintenance
   factors.

9. *Ward Atmosphere Scale* (WAS; Moos, 1974). A measure of perceived program orientation and organization and of ward interpersonal relationships.
10. *Work Environment Scale* (WES; Moos, 1981). A measure of workplace interpersonal relationships, orientation, and work stress.

There have also been developed a number of health-specific measures that might prove useful, depending upon the targets of assessment chosen, for example,

1. *Jenkins Activity Survey* (JAS; Jenkins, Zyzanski, & Rosenman, 1979). A self-report measure of the Type A behavior pattern.
2. *Sickness Impact Profile* (SIP; Bergner, Bobbitt, Carter, & Gilson, 1981). A quality-of-life measure applicable to any disease or disability group.
3. *Arthritis Impact Measurement Scale* (AIMS; Meenan, Gertman, & Mason, 1982). A measure of the effects of arthritis upon functioning and the quality of life.
4. *McGill Pain Questionnaire* (MPQ; Melzack, 1975). A measure of perceived pain intensity and sensory, affective, and cognitive components of pain.
5. *Cornell Medical Index* (CMI; Brodman, Erdman, & Wolff, 1949). A self-report measure of health status.
6. *Dental Anxiety Scale* (Corah, 1969).

Obviously this listing is not exhaustive. We cannot emphasize enough the need for the clinical health psychologist to be aware of the reliability and validity issues specific to each measure *for each usage*. Failure to recognize limits of interpretation of test results is contrary not only to good clinical practice but also to ethical standards, as discussed in chapters 4 and 8.

Observation

Observation of the patient is one of the most fundamental methods of assessment, and it can provide the clinician with information applicable to many of the target areas described in our model. Observation can be unstructured or highly structured. For example, it can occur as part of a general clinical interview or in a more "naturalistic" setting (e.g., a treatment setting involving interactions with nursing staff or response to medical procedures such as burn debridement). Structured observations can include tasks such as role-playing interactions with family, employer, or physician and *in vivo* experiences such as observing cold-stress challenges for Raynaud's disease patients and self-administration of insulin in the diabetic. Observations may be made directly by the clinician, by family members, or by health care providers; observations may be audio or video tape recorded. Because this is an obviously reactive measure, the influence of the measurement process on data obtained must be considered in interpretation.

Observations can be quantified by rating methods (e.g., Hamilton Anxiety Scale [Hamilton, 1959]), content analyses (e.g., somatic focus), or frequency scores (e.g., pill counts to determine compliance), among other methods. The clinician may also collect impressions in an effort to generate hypotheses for more precise testing. It is especially useful to compare direct observation of behavior to others' perceptions of the behavior or to the patient's own perception of his or her behavior (e.g., the "demanding patient"). Reasons for the lack of correlation could be clinically very meaningful, and thus help target areas for intervention.

Psychophysiological Measures

Psychophysiology refers to the "scientific study by nonsurgical means of the interrelationships between psychological processes and physiological systems in humans" (Cacioppo, Petty, & Marshall-Goodell, 1985, p. 264). Psychophysiological measures are designed to provide information about biologic events (e.g., heart rate) or consequences of biologic events (e.g., skin temperature). They can also be used to provide feedback to the individual and thus serve as psychological interventions (e.g., biofeedback).

The biologic events of most interest to the clinical health psychologist include skin conductance, muscle tension, skin temperature, blood pressure, heart rate, and respiratory activity. Parameters of interest include average resting levels, within-subject variability, and response of the measure to differing conditions (e.g., stress, relaxation, resting, imagery, specified activities).

Although psychophysiological profiles have been increasingly utilized (e.g., Berman & Johnson, 1985), the current lack of clinical predictive value renders them, in our opinion, less useful in the initial stages of a diagnostic workup. For example, lack of correlation between level of muscle tension and the diagnosis of "muscle contraction headache" has been found repeatedly (Philips, 1978; Sutton & Belar, 1982). However, once the decision is made to undertake treatment, psychophysiological profiling could become a very important part of the treatment process.

To undertake psychophysiological measurements, the clinician needs to have expertise in, among other things, bioelectric and physiological processes, instrumentation and recording techniques, signal processing methods, and potential artifacts and confounds. We believe that advances in telemetric and ambulatory monitoring will increase the ecological validity of these kinds of measures, with a subsequent increase in clinical usage in the near future.

Archival Data

Literature reviews of diseases, including cause, symptoms, course, prevention, treatment, and psychological components, can provide archival data that can be useful in the assessment process. Reviews of previous medical and psychiatric charts are an additional source of information for the clinical health psychologist. Although these records are not always easily obtained, the clinician will find the information contained within them invaluable in providing a historical perspective of the patient and her or his problem.

It might also be necessary to consult archival data when assessing the potential impact on the problem of various environmental variables, such as the health care system and the sociocultural environment. Hospital policies, insurance coverages, legislation relating to disability, laws regulating the practice of health care provision, and employers' policies all need to be understood in order to develop an adequate conceptualization of the case.

Other Methods

There are a number of other methods of assessment available to the clinical health psychologist that could prove useful under specified conditions. For example, pedometers might provide fruitful information about activity level and thus be especially useful in problems such as chronic lower back pain. Spirometric measures of pulmonary functioning can be utilized as dependent measures in work with asthmatics. Smoking behavior can be measured by thiocyanate levels in blood serum, urine, and saliva. Skin-fold thickness, as an indirect measure of body fat, might be useful in dealing with problems of obesity. Sleep electroencephalograms are useful in assessing sleep disorders. Body weight can be a useful measure of compliance to dietary restrictions in hemodialysis patients. The range of other methods of assessment is limited only by the uniqueness of the problem and the creativity of the professional.

ACHIEVING THE GOALS OF ASSESSMENT: UNDERSTANDING THE PATIENT

At the end of the assessment process, the clinician will have an understanding of the patient in his or her physical and social environment, the patient's relevant strengths and weaknesses, the evidence for psychopathology, the nature of the disease and treatment regimen, and the coping skills being utilized. After integrating all of the information, the clinician should be able to answer the following seven questions. These questions have been derived from Moos (1977), who delineated these areas as the major adaptive tasks to be accomplished by any patient with a medical illness. The relative importance of answers to each question in determining the overall status of the patient of course varies, dependent upon the understanding developed through assessment of the previously mentioned targets.

1. How is the patient dealing with pain, incapacitation, and other symptoms?
2. How is the patient dealing with the hospital environment and the special treatment procedures?
3. Is the patient developing and maintaining adequate relationships with health care staff?
4. Is the patient preserving reasonable emotional balance?
5. Is the patient preserving a satisfactory self-image and maintaining a sense of competence and mastery?
6. Is the patient preserving relationships with family and friends?
7. How is the patient preparing for an uncertain future?

In conclusion, the purpose of the clinical health psychology assessment is to understand the patient and her or his problem so as to arrive at a treatment strategy or a management decision. One need not be wedded to a particular theory or assessment strategy; indeed, flexibility in this regard is, in our opinion, an asset. However, we do attempt to adhere to the biopsychosocial conceptual framework.

SUGGESTED READINGS

Karoly, P. (Ed.). (1985). *Measurement strategies in health psychology*. New York: John Wiley & Sons.

Keefe, F. J., & Blumenthal, J. A. (Eds.). (1982). *Assessment strategies in behavioral medicine*. New York: Grune & Straton.

Prokop, C. K., & Bradley, L. A. (Eds.). (1981). *Medical psychology: Contributions to behavioral medicine*. New York: Academic Press.

Chapter 7
Intervention Strategies in Clinical Health Psychology

In chapter 6 we presented our framework for applying the biopsycho-social model to the assessment process in clinical health psychology. At the end of that process, the clinician should be aware of potential problem areas for the patient and related environmental contributors, and of the variety of resources available. The next step, then, is to translate these findings into some plan of intervention. Clinical health psychology intervention can also be conceptualized using our model, although the focus changes to working in present and future time realms. Many of the targets of assessment described in Table 6.1 can also become targets for intervention. As with assessment, there is significant overlap among the various targets. Intervention at any one level almost always affects functioning and intervention in other areas. This issue will be discussed further after a general outline of each domain of intervention is presented.

PATIENT TARGETS

At the level of the patient, the clinician can attempt intervention in biological, affective, cognitive, or behavioral domains.

Biological

Treatment strategies in this domain are designed to directly change actual physiological responses involved in the disorder. Examples include biofeedback for fecal incontinence and relaxation for hypertension. One can also intervene in an attempt to control specific symptoms associated with the disease or its treatment (e.g., hypnosis for pain control, desensitization for the anticipatory nausea associated with chemotherapy). Medical interventions typically occur within this domain, and their interactive effects with simultaneous psycho-physiological treatment must be constantly monitored (e.g., biofeedback for relaxation training while the patient is on prn benzodiazepine medication).

Affective

In the affective domain, one might focus on such emotional states as anxiety, depression, or hostility. For instance, the clinician could provide such interventions as stress inoculation to decrease anxiety about an upcoming medical procedure, cognitive behavioral treatment for depression, and anger management for Type A behavior pattern.

Cognitive

Interventions in this domain involve providing information in a psychoeducational approach or changing the manner in which a patient conceptualizes a problem. As examples, one might maximize placebo effects of medical or psychological treatments, provide sensory and procedural information about upcoming diagnostic procedures, challenge unrealistic expectations about sexual activity post penile prosthesis surgery, and utilize existential psychotherapy to facilitate the development of a philosophy of life consistent with adaptive coping.

Behavioral

Treatment in this area includes changing the patient's overt behaviors and usually involves using principles of social learning theory. Thus, the clinician might design a self-monitoring program to enhance compliance with hypertension medication, teach assertion skills to facilitate communication with the patient's physician, develop a behavior change program to modify behavioral health-risk factors (such as smoking or weight), or consult in the training of the patient in such self-management skills as insulin injections and stoma care.

ENVIRONMENTAL TARGETS

Targets need not be patient-focused, however, as the clinician could decide that an environmental intervention is either necessary for change or easier to accomplish. Once again the environmental units include (a) the family, (b) the health care system, and (c) the sociocultural context. Intervention within each of these units might include physical, affective, cognitive, or behavioral domains as defined earlier.

Family

Interventions aimed at the physical aspects of the family environment include the redesign of living space in accordance with patient limitations (e.g., specified order of spices in the cabinet for the blind housekeeper) and referrals to social agencies for financial resources. In the affective realm, the clinician could utilize supportive therapy to help family members deal with anxiety about the patient's illness. In the cognitive arena, the clinician could facilitate more realistic expectations through the provision of accurate information, or he or she might use family therapy to work through potential misattributions of the cause of the patient's illness. In terms of family members' behavior, it might be necessary to train individuals to give appropriate support, or to develop a contingency-management program so that the family does not unwittingly reinforce unnecessary sick-role behavior.

Health Care System

The health care system is a frequent target of intervention. One of the most important aspects is the physical domain within which services are provided. Interventions can be as simple as suggestions to increase orientation of intensive-care-unit patients through time prompts and of chronically ill patients through the availability of calendars. Privacy is very important to patients, but is often neglected in the health care system. The authors are aware of one radiation-therapy waiting room situated in a busy hallway, where patients with disfigured appearances often sit uncomfortably, subjected to the stares or grimaces of hospital visitors. Environmental design that is sensitive to and respectful of patient needs can produce a more relaxing, less anxiety-provoking, atmosphere; thus, music, ceiling art, and bubbling fish tanks are increasingly used in waiting and treatment rooms. The clinical health psychologist working within an institutional context often needs to adopt an advocacy role to bring about these kinds of health care system interventions. Many of the physical environment manipulations are not costly or difficult to implement.

In the affective realm of the health care system, the clinician might also need to work with medical and nursing staffs concerning their feelings about a specific patient in order to facilitate a therapeutic relationship between caregivers and patient (e.g., reframing demanding patient behavior as an attempt to exert control in the face of enforced, threatening dependency). In our experience, it is not uncommon for staff to express angry feelings toward a patient (such as the suicidal patient on a medical unit) in a passive–aggressive manner that tends to foster retaliatory acting-out in the patient. This, of course, sets up a cyclical behavior pattern, which can become exceedingly severe if it is not interrupted.

In the cognitive arena, clinical health psychologists continually find themselves in the role of teacher, as in most interactions they attempt to increase the knowledge of other health care providers about the psychological aspects of health, illness, and patient care. This education also involves dispelling myths and providing correct information about various psychological disorders that present as part of, or simultaneously with, a medical problem.

We suggest that the majority of communications back to referral sources include explicit recommendations about how the health care provider's own behaviour could facilitate treatment of the patient. Interventions aimed at the behavior of health care providers include instructions to increase attention for well behavior; provide medication on a fixed interval rather than on an as-needed basis for chronic pain patients; have only one physician responsible for coordination of care; check for patient understanding of treatment instructions; and to train the patient in self-care when possible, even when hospitalized, to maximize a sense of mastery and self-control in the patient. Advocacy for progressive health care policies might also be warranted (e.g., development of interdisciplinary teams).

Sociocultural Context

Often, only certain aspects of the sociocultural context are available for immediate intervention. For example, it is possible to intervene in the social network and thus use its resources to the benefit of the patient. We have counseled friends of patients on ways to facilitate coping in patients, and have given them information about the grieving process that enhanced their understanding. We have also worked with employers in designing a gradual return to work and resumption of activity for the patient recovering from a serious illness or learning to live with a chronic pain problem. (Interestingly, one major health care system does not permit such a gradual return to work of its own employees. Instead the employee must be released to return to "100% functioning" if the worker is to be reinstated, a frequently doomed approach in terms of principles of rehabilitation.)

Other aspects of the sociocultural environment are the subject of rather long-term interventions by clinical health psychologists and are perhaps as important when considering the future quality of patient care. Such "interventions" include contributing to the body of knowledge about effective diagnostic and treatment strategies via clinical research, serving as volunteers with public information groups to defuse cultural myths and stereotypes, working toward behavioral health legislation (e.g., controls on smoking in the workplace), and participating in governmental policy-making regarding health care provision.

CHOOSING TARGETS FOR INTERVENTION

When deciding among the areas of intervention, one must take into account the effects of any given intervention on other targets, the appropriateness of goals for intervention, issues of patient and staff cooperation, and cost–benefit issues.

Interrelationships of Interventions

Just as information obtained about one target of assessment can influence the interpretation of information obtained about another, so are the targets of intervention interrelated. Interventions aimed at one target can have positive or negative effects on other areas of functioning or ongoing treatments. For instance, in the positive realm, a patient who is treated for chronic headaches using relaxation and biofeedback approaches might find that she or he needs to take less of the prn pain medication, feels less depressed, notes an improvement in family relationships, and has increased her or his activity level. Thus, a positive adaptive cycle of improvement has been initiated by treatment aimed primarily at the headache problem.

However, one must be particularly concerned about negative effects that any area of intervention might have on other areas. For example, let us assume that the initial decision is made to increase self-management skills (e.g., self-catheterization) in order to promote more independent functioning. Success in this endeavor is likely to bring with it an increased sense of control over bodily functions, which is usually associated with a reduction in anxiety and a decrease in autonomic nervous system arousal. However, self-catheterization can also be associated with an increase in family members' fears about adequate treatment of the patient, because a professional is no longer performing the technique. Or family members might be repulsed by the nature of the procedure occuring at home and subsequently discourage the patient's attempts. In this situation, the primary intervention might have short-lived success, unless these other areas are monitored and addressed.

In another example, the use of relaxation training to help manage stress in a patient with diabetes can produce shifts in insulin needs that warrant close medical attention so as to not produce unstable diabetes (Rosenbaum, 1983). Inattention to these potential effects when designing an intervention program can result in treatment failures or unexpected negative side effects. In our experience, it is extremely rare that the clinician can focus solely on a single target for intervention.

In summary, a primary factor in choosing a target is the understanding of its interrelationships with other blocks in the model. This understanding is obtained through knowledge of the specific problem area, the research on the various interventions available, and a firm grounding in the clinical process of behavior change.

Appropriateness of Goals

Another aspect to consider when choosing targets for intervention is the determination of a realistic and attainable goal for treatment. This often involves taking into account the likelihood that the targeted goal is amenable to treatment. For example, the care-seeking behavior of Munchausen and polysurgical patients is notoriously unresponsive to nearly all forms of psychological intervention. These patients also tend to elicit a good deal of anger on the part of health care providers. Thus, it is sometimes wiser to target interventions toward preventing the inappropriate taking out of this anger on the patient by the staff and protecting the patient from unnecessary medical procedures rather than toward the psychological issues related to the help-seeking behavior itself. It is important to explicitly specify the target(s) of intervention and to operationalize them in order to permit evaluation of change (e.g., do not set as a goal "improve compliance" but rather "take medication three times per day with meals"). Clear articulation of targets is also critical to obtaining informed consent for treatment. For example, we once saw a young woman on an orthopedic ward who, subsequent to a bicycle accident, had both legs in traction. She was not eating sufficiently to permit bone mending and engaged in constant conflicts with nursing staff. Further evaluation revealed the presence of anorexia nervosa, which the patient denied and for which she refused treatment. However, she did consent to a focused treatment goal of obtaining sufficient nutrients to permit bone growth.

Related to the issue of appropriate goal setting is the importance of understanding whether the goal of intervention is cure or the facilitation of coping. A cure is not unreasonable to expect in some areas, but much of what we do in clinical practice is done to promote coping. Often the clinician needs to maintain a delicate balance between hope and positive expectations that can facilitate treatment and the reality of the situation that could suggest a poor prognosis.

Cooperation of the Patient and Staff

The choice of a particular intervention often depends heavily on the cooperation of patient, staff, or both, and its feasibility in ameliorating the current problem. One can spend hours designing a very powerful treatment program that depends on the staff's executing various components, only to have it fail miserably when an uncooperative (or already overburdened) staff must execute it. The authors are reminded of a situation in which a relatively straightforward behavioral program was designed to address the acting out behavior of a girl with a closed-head injury. Theoretically, the program should have worked, but inconsistent application by the staff, lack of commitment, and communication problems assured its failure. When designing an intervention that requires staff involvement, one must take into account such things as their willingness and ability to participate, the simplicity and ease of treatment administration, and the potential for sabotage or misapplication. Educating staff about the treatment and giving them an understandable rationale for its implementation are important.

Cost–benefit Analysis

As discussed before, in deciding among intervention strategies in clinical health psychology, one must consider not only the information obtained during the assessment process (review Table 6.1) but also certain aspects of the intervention strategies themselves, specifically their costs and benefits. Unfortunately, these decisions often cannot be made on an empirical basis in the practice of psychology, given the lack of adequately designed clinical trials for many of our therapeutic strategies. Nevertheless, the clinician should consider issues of treatment efficacy, efficiency, durability, generality, convenience, cost, side effects, and clinician competence.

The clinical health psychologist needs to understand how effective the treatment strategy is in terms of absolute change in the target of intervention. In addition, one must address the following questions in the decision-making process: How efficient is the intervention in terms of time involved and effort expended? For how long are the results expected to last? What percentage of patients with similar problems can be expected to respond using the intervention (this is especially important in deciding upon strategies to be utilized in a group program)? How convenient or inconvenient to the patient and to his or her environment (including the therapist) is the treatment? What is the cost of the intervention? What are the side effects of the particular strategies or the program to be utilized? And finally, how competent is the clinician in utilizing the particular intervention strategy? This type of self-questioning can help in the process of deciding among several alternative intervention possibilities.

INTERVENTION STRATEGIES

Once the targets of intervention have been chosen, the clinician must select a strategy of intervention. In this process of selection, we encourage flexibility, without rigid adherence to any one or two particular strategies.

Historically, the development of psychological interventions for medical–surgical patients has moved from general, broadband techniques to those methods designed to address more narrowly and specifically defined targets. We shall follow this format in describing the more commonly used therapeutic intervention strategies in the practice of clinical health psychology, giving examples of usage and references for further study. Although the following techniques are discussed as single-treatment entities, it is recognized that many of these procedures are used in combination in actual practice.

Placebo Effect

The placebo effect might be the simplest behavioral change procedure in common use (Agras, 1984). It refers to changes in behavior that occur because of the patient's expectations and faith that a particular treatment will produce the desired change. It can influence all target domains and is undoubtedly a part of all treatments. It is particularly powerful in pain control (where it has been linked to increased circulating endorphins) and can be used in such problems as conversion reactions (e.g., using EMG biofeedback to "shape" movement behavior in nonorganic paralysis). The reader is referred to Shapiro (1971) and Frank (1973) for a complete review of literature on the placebo effect.

Supportive Counseling

Physicians have historically attempted to support patients by reassuring them regarding illness and treatment procedures. Prokop and Bradley (1981) used the term *psychological support* to define this rather vague, nonspecific form of psychotherapeutic intervention directed toward amelioration of the patient's psychological distress. This type of treatment can involve individual or family meetings or consist of organized support groups. Further, supportive psychotherapy can be clinician-based or network-based, depending on the nature of the problem and the availability of community resources. Other health care providers and paraprofessionals can be trained to provide supportive counseling and thus become valuable resources to the practicing psychologist.

Individual and family approaches. These types of interventions are generally based on a short-term treatment model and focus on helping the patient and her or his family cope successfully with psychologically threatening information or procedures. This can be done by encouraging active participation in medical decisions, establishing a good patient–therapist relationship, and assuring the patient that feelings of anxiety and de-pression are normal (Gruen, 1975). The clinician should never underesti-mate the power of a pat on the back or a squeeze of the hand, procedures unlikely to be practiced in traditional clinical psychology.

Support groups. Group discussion typically allows an opportunity for patients with similar illnesses or problems to meet with one another to discuss their concerns, anxieties, and coping strategies, as well as to obtain information. Examples include preparation-for-childbirth groups, postmastectomy groups, arthritis self-help groups, and groups for AIDS family members. Such groups can have a designated leader or be leader-less, and they typically meet on a specified hospital ward or in an outpatient clinic. There is a wide range of local and national associations that target specific disease populations and that an provide information about such groups in a particular community (see appendix C).

Comment. Because the clinical health psychologist frequently utilizes active approaches to treatment, the clinician might feel that supportive therapy does not represent "real therapy." If the clinician can bear in mind that supportive intervention requires an accurate perception of the patient's coping skills and empathy, which can revive a sense of endur-ance (Greenberg, 1986), he or she is less likely to become frustrated in the course of this work.

Verbal Psychotherapy

There are a variety of approaches toward verbal psychotherapy (e.g., analytic, cognitive–behavioral, rational–emotive, directive, systems-oriented), some of which will be discussed in this chapter. Psychotherapy can be symptom-specific, general in focus, or a combination of both. Psychotherapy has been shown to reduce medical utilization, to decrease post-surgery use of narcotics, to reduce symptoms associated with peptic ulcer, and to enhance coping following myocardial infarction (see Agras, 1984).

Education and Information

In clinical health psychology treatment, education about the biopsycho-social model and its specific application to the patient and his or her problem is an essential ingredient. In addition, provision of information is necessary to obtain informed consent for any treatment and to ensure compliance with medical regimens. It is fundamental to the whole field of health education with which clinical health psychologists often interact. Information has also been utilized as a specific intervention to promote coping with illness and with stressful medical procedures. There are two types of information: procedural and sensory. *Procedural* refers to information about aspects of the medical procedure itself, and *sensory* refers to information regarding sensations the patient feels during or after the procedure. Although sensory information appears, in general, to be a more important aspect of preparation, interactions among kind of information, individual coping styles, and level of initial anxiety have been found. The belief that more is better is naive; some patients actually do worse with more information. The clinician must have a strong background in this literature in order to practice effectively (see Gil, 1984; Kendall & Watson, 1981).

Crisis Intervention

Life events that overwhelm the patient's ability to cope or those that reinstate earlier conflicts are apt to create crisis situations. In the practice of clinical health psychology, the psychologist is likely to face a sizable percentage of patients whose lives are in crisis. Often these crises are centered around personal or professional losses from illness or death of a family member. However, the actual crisis is not necessarily related to health issues and could represent any number of developmental or accidental events. Whatever the precipitating event, the psychologist needs to have an understanding of crisis intervention as a therapeutic technique and be aware of the immediate goals of crisis counseling.

Korchin (1976, p. 507) listed three primary goals of crisis intervention (a) to relieve the patient's present psychological distress (e.g. anxiety, hopelessness, confusion), (b) to restore the patient to his or her previous level of functioning, and (c) to help the patient and significant others learn what personal actions and community resources are available. In practice, these goals are accomplished by acknowledging the patient's thoughts, feelings, and behaviors; helping the patient to stay problem-focused by exploring alternative explanations and solutions; emphasizing the patient's strengths in coping with previous life events; mobilizing additional resources; and providing the patient with necessary information and advice, as appropriate. In working with problems of grief, it is important not to build the patient's defenses too quickly, in order to avoid a potentially maladaptive grief reaction. Crisis intervention for the clinical health psychologist often involves working with family members, significant others, and health care providers, as well as with the identified patient.

Relaxation Training Procedures

Perhaps the most well recearched clinical health psychology intervention strategy is relaxation training. Reviews of the literature attest to its usefulness in the treatment of hypertension, tension and migraine headache, insomnia, irritable bowel syndrome, Raynaud's disease, pain tolerance, preparation for stressful medical procedures, and nausea (Agras, 1984; Feuerstein, Labbé, & Kuczmierczyk, 1986). Because this training is considered the "aspirin of behavioral medicine" (Russo, Bird, & Masek, 1980), we are hard pressed to conceive of a practicing clinical health psychologist who does not have expertise in one or more of the techniques to be discussed, all of which have as their goal the reduction of physiological arousal. Although relaxation strategies were originally proposed as interventions in the physiological state of the patient, it is apparent that they also provide interventions in the affective and cognitive domains because they enhance a sense of mastery and competence.

Relaxation strategies have in common that they are all easily learned and easily administered by the clinician. The procedures to be discussed are diaphragmatic breathing, progressive muscle relaxation, and autogenic relaxation training.

Diaphragmatic breathing. Diaphragmatic breathing is a simple form of relaxation exercise that teaches the patient to breathe through his or her diaphragm (see McKay, Davis, & Fanning, 1981 for training instructions in this and the strategies described next). Although frequently used prior to beginning a more in-depth relaxation exercise, this technique is also commonly used by itself to break a conditioned response to a stressor.

Progressive muscle relaxation (PMR). Progressive muscle relaxation is based on the principle that relaxation (relaxed muscles) has physiological accompaniments which are the opposite of those of anxiety (i.e., physiological tension). Jacobson (1939) developed this technique by teaching patients to intentionally tense, then relax, various muscle groups throughout the body. Patients could thereby familiarize themselves with the sometimes subtle distinction between relaxed and tense states—a form of discrimination learning. Variations use different muscle groupings in the training process. This particular procedure is widely used in the practice of clinical health psychology, and is particularly useful for those patients who are unaware of their levels of body tension. The following example demonstrates the usefulness of PMR in training a patient to relax her neck muscles during conversation.

Mrs. N. was a 39-year-old Caucasian woman who experienced muscle tension in her neck with accompanying strained, raspy speech. She entered psychological treatment to learn to decrease the neck cramps she experienced at the end of each work day and to improve the quality of her speech.

The patient was initially trained in basic PMR exercises. Following several sessions of total-body relaxation training, the patient was instructed to specifically focus her attention on the muscles in her neck and throat. After several additional relaxation training sessions, the patient developed awareness of tension cues that signaled to her the need to relax before the tension became problematic. Through increased sensitivity to physiological processes, the patient became better able to control her levels of tension, the quality of her speech, and her neck cramping.

Although most patients are capable of tensing and relaxing various muscle groups, it might be necessary for the clinician to slightly modify the standard procedures to accommodate certain types of patients: those with chronic back low back pain or spinal fusions, with paraplegia or quadraplegia, with arthritis, or with limited mobility.

Autogenic relaxation training. Autogenic training (Schultz & Luthe, 1969) can create a very deep state of relaxation through the use of positive self-statements directed at various body parts and suggesting sensations of warmth, heaviness, calmness, and so forth.

> Ms. O. was very anxious about an impending gynecologic examination, which was designed to determine the cause of her infertility and would involve some painful procedures. She had a history of becoming so upset during even routine pelvic examinations that she subsequently had to miss work, needing a day to recover from her trauma.

The patient was trained in autogenic relaxation techniques that she would be able to utilize while lying quietly during the exam. In addition, a number of preparatory procedures, including guided imagery and coping self-statements, were utilized. The patient utilized the autogenic phrases throughout the procedure and coped successfully without incident.

Comment. When considering relaxation therapies, it is noteworthy that, like aspirin, they have sometimes been used indiscriminately with the naive notion that they are good for everyone and everything. Any technique that has such potential benefit must also be assumed to have potential harm. Although there is insufficient attention in the general psychological literature to negative psychological side effects, relaxation training and related procedures have been noted to produce increased anxiety, shifting insulin needs and diabetic instability, hypotension in the elderly, and flooding of intrusive thoughts and impulses (e.g., Heide &

Borkovec, 1984; Seeburg & DeBoer, 1980). Careful pretreatment evaluation, proper monitoring, and appropriate modification of procedures are critical to good practice. The reader is referred to the following references for transcripts of various relaxation techniques and related discussions: Bernstein and Borkovec (1973); Davis, Eshelman, and McKay (1980); Turk, Meichenbaum, and Genest (1983).

Imagery

Imagery makes use of the private inner world of the patient through created images, imagination, and focused awareness. The use of imagery may be directed at general relaxation and anxiety reduction, symptom treatment, and behavioral change.

Guided imagery. Samuels and Samuels (1975) described the positive physiological and psychological effects of visual imagery. Patients are asked to visualize, in minute detail, a scene that they consider to be relaxing. As the scene becomes clearer, the patient begins to relax.

Other forms of imagery utilize all of the body's senses and ask patients to project themselves into the scene being imagined rather than just watching the scene before them. In these exercises, the patient's mind plays a very active role through imaged re-creation of certain sights, smells, sounds, tastes, and touch. We use this technique in pain management as a means of recalling a pain-free episode in the patient's life and of re-creating the associated sense of well-being. We also use guided imagery to prepare for stressful medical procedures.

Covert sensitization. Covert sensitization is a procedure developed by Cautela (1967) that applies the laws of classical conditioning to imagery. Use of this technique has primarily been directed toward extinguishing previously learned maladaptive behaviors, such as smoking or overeating. This is accomplished by associating a learned habit (smoking) with very detailed and unpleasant, obnoxious, and repulsive stimuli that are imagined, such as burning eyes, nausea, or sore throat. By pairing the habit with a visualized noxious response, presumably the habit will no longer be associated with pleasure.

Comment. Imagery is an ideal relaxation and symptom reduction treatment for many patients, as it does not require active movement or special equipment. However, the successful use of these techniques also requires a moderate ability to concentrate for a sustained period of time, and the ability to implement a certain degree of fantasy. There are some patients who report that they are not good imagers, but this is a skill that can be trained. However, patients who are rigidly controlled cognitively or who lack adequate reality testing are probably not good candidates for these techniques. Pain patients who are taking high doses of narcotic medication often find these exercises difficult, if not impossible, due to their impaired concentration levels.

Hypnosis

Although well-controlled clinical trials are absent, hypnosis has been reported useful in the treatment of pain, skin diseases, warts, and coping with chronic disease. Goals are usually to produce direct physiological changes, to change the perception of a symptom, to foster general relaxation, or to facilitate insight related to a particular symptom (see reviews by DePiano and Selzberg [1979] and Weisenberg [1978]). Self-hypnosis as described by LeCron (1970) is quite similar to a therapist-induced trance but transfers responsibility for trance induction and awakening to the patient. This technique has been particularly useful for uncovering unconscious material that has led to a maladaptive symptom.

We are aware of one case in which total body palsy in a young adult was cured through the use of both hypnosis and self-hypnosis. Hypnosis helped the therapist identify the emotional factors related to onset of the symptom (an urge to hit her father at the onset of an argument and the patient's effort at control by holding back, resulting in a trembling hand that later spread to the entire body). The patient was then taught self-hypnosis, so that she could voluntarily control the symptoms by being able to both produce the palsy and eliminate it.

Biofeedback

The primary goal of biofeedback training is to teach the patient voluntary control over physiological processes. The reader is referred to a review of the clinical biofeedback literature for further study in this area (Olton & Noonberg, 1980; Ray, Raczynski, Rogers, & Kimball, 1979). Originally thought to be a specific intervention in the physiological realm, more recent analyses have suggested that biofeedback can also be utilized as an intervention in the cognitive and affective domains. Successful training facilitates the patient's perceived control over physiological events, a belief that might play a significant role in treatment outcome. Perceived control and lower autonomic nervous system arousal are also associated with decreased affective states, such as anxiety. The technology associated with biofeedback intervention makes it quite acceptable as a psychological intervention with patients in our electronically oriented society.

The two most commonly used forms of biofeedback include EMG and skin temperature. EMG feedback is useful for educating patients about the level of muscle tension present in selected muscle groups and can thus be useful in musculoskeletal disorders. Fingertip temperature provides an indirect measure of peripheral blood volume and, as such, has been used for disorders associated with vasodilation and vasoconstriction.

In general, these procedures have been utilized for a variety of stress-related and psychophysiological disorders including bruxism, tension headache, anxiety, migraine headache, Raynaud's disease, asthma, chronic pain, and essential hypertension. However, other relaxation-training procedures are often as successful with these problems, and there is little empirical evidence to support a preference for a particular technique such as biofeedback, hypnosis, imagery, or relaxation training, although sophisticated studies considering individual differences have not yet been completed. Experienced clinicians engage in complex decision-making in their choices. As Belar and Kibrick (1986) noted in their discussion of the use of EMG biofeedback in the treatment of chronic back pain, the clinician might choose this technique for one of three reasons, when working with this population: (a) to produce a specific physiological change such as equalization of muscle tension in the back or reduction of spasm; (b) to train in general relaxation which is associated with increased pain tolerance and decreased distress; or (c) to facilitate "physiological insight" as the patient learns about relationships between psychological and physiological processes.

More specific uses of biofeedback in clinical health psychology include use of feedback about (a) heart rate to control cardiac arrhythmias; (b) the anal spinchter to control fecal incontinence; (c) airway resistance for asthma; (d) muscular functioning for neuromuscular reeducation, dysphagia, and torticollis, among other problems; (e) brain wave patterns for epilepsy; and (f) blood pressure for postural hypotension in patients with spinal cord injuries (see reviews in Olton & Noonberg, 1980). A very new and exciting application is the use of ear oximetry feedback during pursed-lip breathing, to increase blood oxygenation in chronic obstructive pulmonary disease patients (Tiep, Burns, Kao, Madison, & Herrera, 1986).

Comment. It should be noted that many of the applications of biofeedback still lack strong empirical support for their efficacy in general patient populations. In addition, use of these techniques requires specialized training in bioelectric signal processing, psychophysiology, and electrical equipment. The Biofeedback Certification Institute of America certifies therapists for practice in this area.

Systematic Desensitization

Systematic desensitization as developed by Wolpe (1958) is designed to teach the patient to emit a behavior that is inconsistent with anxiety. In the practice of clinical health psychology, this procedure is often used to reduce patients' fears and accompanying anxiety concerning certain medical or dental procedures. As with modeling, this procedure can be performed either imaginally or *in vivo*, and it usually involves a combination of both. Consider the following example:

> Mrs P. was a 56-year-old Black female with known hypertension who had been prescribed antihypertensive medications. She was referred by her cardiologist for evaluation and treatment because she had developed a phobia related to blood pressure monitoring. Each time she visited her doctor's office for blood pressure readings, she became increasingly anxious and thus highly aroused cardiovascularly.

This patient was treated using systematic desensitization in an effort to help her become less reactive to blood pressure monitoring. A hierarchy of progressively anxiety-producing circumstances associated with taking her blood pressure was first elicited. The patient was then instructed in PMR techniques. While relaxed, Mrs. P. practiced imagined scenes of increasing difficulty. Instruments, measurements, and health care professionals were then gradually introduced, allowing the patient to adapt to each set of circumstances before proceeding to the next highest level.

Systematic desensitization has also been utilized to decrease fears of childbirth, to deal with needle phobias and excessive dependence upon nebulizers, and to facilitate reentry into public settings by burned or surgically-deformed patients.

Modeling

Based on the theory of observational learning (Bandura, 1969), modeling provides a means of facilitating the learning of adaptive behaviors. This can be accomplished through either *in vivo* (direct observation) or imaginal (filmed or covert) techniques. Modeling is an important method for teaching patients necessary skills that might be required to meet the demands of their illnesses (e.g. teaching self-injection of insulin), and it also reduces patient anxiety in preparation for stressful medical procedures. Melamed and her colleagues have demonstrated repeatedly that filmed modeling to prepare children for medical and dental procedures, as well as for hospitalization, can be very useful in reducing anxiety and behavioral problems (Melamed & Siegel, 1980). Additionally, this technique is useful for interventions directed at patient–staff and staff–staff issues. Finally, the clinician himself or herself can model more therapeutic or facilitative interactions.

Comment. The clinical health psychologist should be aware of the negative effects of poor models. Consider the following example:

> Mrs. K. was a 59-year-old Caucasian woman admitted to the hospital for a colostomy. As part of standard procedure, she was interviewed prior to the surgery and initially appeared to be coping quite well with the information presented to her. On the day of the scheduled surgery (3 days past the planned date, due to a slight elevation in her temperature), Mrs. K. was considerably anxious, fearful of dying, and reluctant to sign the surgical form for informed consent.

Upon interviewing this patient, the clinical health psychologist learned that the other woman sharing Mrs. K.'s room had recently undergone the same operation and was now experiencing considerable pain and discomfort secondary to a postsurgical infection. Given the similarities in age and diagnosis, the patient had been unwittingly provided with an effective negative role model. In this example, staff had failed to consider the impact of one patient on another. A move to another room helped alleviate some of Mrs. K.'s concerns.

Skills Training and Behavioral Rehearsal

Skills training can incorporate modeling, role playing, and behavioral rehearsal. Patients can learn specific skills that can enhance their psychological and physical adjustment. In the practice of clinical health psychology, the most commonly taught skills are in the area of self-assertion. Whether in a formal or informal manner, we frequently find ourselves helping patients become more assertive, particularly when dealing with medical personnel.

Specific tasks that are taught include learning to formulate and to ask direct questions of physicians, requesting special privileges and giving justifications, requesting privacy during physical exams, learning to appropriately inquire as to alternative treatments, and requesting a second medical opinion. We frequently encourage patients to write down questions to ask their physicians and to obtain written answers if necessary. It is well known that patients can lose up to 50% of the information to which they are exposed during an office visit (see Ley, 1982, for review). We also encourage physicians to request that patients repeat back to them an understanding of the problem and the recommended treatment plan. This simple procedure eliminates many miscommunications and unmet expectations.

Other targets of skills training include the learning of specific behaviors necessary for good health care or rehabilitation. Although clinical health psychologists might not directly teach these skills, they frequently interact with other health care providers (e.g. occupational therapists, physical therapists, speech therapists, nurses) to address either the emotional aspects or the learning principles associated with acquiring new and often "unnatural" skills. Examples of these skills are proper care of surgical stomas, bowel and bladder care following spinal cord injury, and home dialysis.

Contingency Management

As a treatment strategy, the goal of contingency management is to increase adaptive behaviors and to decrease those that are not. Positive reinforcement, negative reinforcement, punishment, response cost, extinction, and shaping procedures can all be used to accomplish this goal. Examples of positive reinforcement include the awarding of prizes to children for adherence to dietary regimens while on hemodialysis (Magreb & Papadopoulou, 1977), the insurance industry's reduction of premiums for nonsmokers, and the use of physician time to reward appropriate health care utilization. Extinction is commonly used to diminish complaining behavior or behaviors designed to elicit attention for the symptom (e.g., grimaces). An example of negative reinforcement includes the work by Malament, Dunn, and Davis (1975), who used the avoidance of an aversive tone to develop habits of postural push-ups in wheelchair patients to avoid the formation of decubitus ulcers.

Although used much less frequently, punishment has been effective in cases of ruminative vomiting in infants. (Whereas Lang and Melamed [1969] used electric shock, Sajwaj, Libet, and Agras [1974] were successful with a small amount of lemon juice.) The rapid-smoking technique is another example of aversive conditioning (Grimaldi & Lichtenstein, 1969).

A major advantage to this type of treatment is that it can be administered by persons other than the clinical health psychologist. Frequently, nursing personnel or family members are educated as to how to change contingencies affecting patient behavior. For example, in attempting to cope with a demanding patient, ward nurses were advised to visit this bell-ringing patient on a regular basis rather than continue to respond (or not respond) to frequent calls for help. As a result, both nursing personnel and the patient were more satisfied and less frustrated by each other's behavior. Family members can be instructed to increase attention and nurturance for well behavior instead of sick-role behavior. In general, contingency management is a major part of comprehensive pain rehabilitation (i.e., multidisciplinary treatment) and is more fully described in Fordyce (1976).

Comment. Although contingency management is effective under well-controlled conditions, its efficacy is diminished by poorly detailed instructions or lack of follow-up. Family members often unwittingly abandon recommended treatment suggestions because of a temporary, albeit annoying, exacerbation of symptoms when the patient has been put on an extinction schedule (*extinction burst*). Additionally, when staff members are implementing a program, it is important to insure that they are not using contingencies to express their anger at a difficult patient. The failure of a contingency management program is often attributable to the clinician's failure to adequately assess the "ABCs" (antecedents, behaviors, and consequences) of the planned intervention.

Self-Monitoring and Cueing

Because of the reactive nature of self-monitoring, the use of patient diaries can be an effective means of intervention as well as of assessment and tracking of treatment efficacy. Simply recording eating, smoking, and compliance behaviors often brings about changes in the desired directions.

Other means of self-monitoring include the use of external or internal cues as a signal to institute a behavior. Patients with complicated medication regimens have been directed to categorize and separate pills into daily doses, using a weekly pill box to help them remember when the next dosage is due. Another example of external cues for self-monitoring includes using time-of-day or environmental prompts as stimuli to perform relaxation exercises.

In the treatment of obesity, patients are taught to attend to internal rather than external cues for signs of hunger and thus self-monitor their food intake. Insulin-dependent diabetic patients can be taught to recognize early warning symptoms of insulin imbalance and make necessary adjustments.

Family members can also participate in these cueing strategies. In addition, the health care system uses these principles when sending appointment reminders as external cues for preventive care.

Comment. Self-monitoring does require a certain degree of self-discipline and commitment to change. Patients who are ambivalent regarding behavioral change are not likely to do well with this procedure unless it is presented in combination with other forms of intervention. Self-monitoring can also be used sometimes as a method of assessing commitment to treatment.

Cognitive Strategies

There are a variety of interventions that utilize cognitive strategies to effect behavioral change. These include the use of distraction, calming self-statements, and cognitive restructuring. In attention-diversion or distraction procedures, patients are taught to direct their attention away from unpleasant events. Use of pleasant imagery, difficult mental tasks (serial 7s backward; reciting the States of the Union in alphabetical order), counting aloud, and focusing attention on other neutral stimuli (counting holes in ceiling tiles) are examples of this process.

Patients can also be taught to silently or softly talk to themselves, utilizing calming, relaxing, and reassuring statements. These statments could emphasize the temporary nature of a discomfort (e.g., "this pain will not last", "I only have 5 minutes to go"), be directed at maintaining low physiological arousal (e.g., "stay calm", "stay relaxed", "breathe"), or be directed toward preservation of self-image (e.g., "I am a strong and worthwhile person", "It's OK to feel uncomfortable", "I can cope with this").

Cognitive restructing is a generic term that describes a variety of procedures, including stress-inoculation training (Meichenbaum, 1977), rational–emotive therapy (Ellis, 1962), cognitive therapy (Beck, Rush, Shaw & Emery, 1979), and problem-solving training (Goldfried & Davison, 1976). As described by Turk et al. (1983), these procedures educate the patient regarding the relationships among thoughts, feelings, and behaviors and help patients replace self-defeating cognitions with adaptive thoughts. McKay et al. (1981) provide detailed instructions in applying many of these techniques.

The list of intervention strategies we have provided is not exhaustive, yet skills in those areas mentioned would prepare the psychologist for beginning practice. In general, these intervention strategies are not used in isolation. For example, stress inoculation is an example of a treatment package that incorporates a variety of strategies. Further, these "generic" strategies need to be adapted for each patient on the basis of the particular disorder and the presentation of the patient's issues.

It is also noteworthy that a number of these strategies are not necessarily patient-focused but can be used either *for* targets within the family, the health care system, or the social network (for example, information, supportive counseling, modeling, skill training, cueing, contingency management) or *by* these environmental agents of change.

The clinical health psychologist cannot be expert in all kinds of possible interventions, nor with all kinds of specific problems likely to be encountered in this broad field, but there are several categories of problems with which the practitioner should have some basic familiarity. These are listed below, along with related references for suggested reading.

SUGGESTED READINGS

Preparation for Stressful Medical Procedures

Gil, K. M. (1984). Coping effectively with invasive medical procedures: A descriptive model. *Clinical Psychology Review, 4*, 339–362.

Kendall, P. C., & Watson, D. (1981). Psychological preparation for stressful medical procedures. In C. K. Prokop & L. A. Bradley (Eds.), *Medical Psychology: Contributions to Behavioral Medicine*. New York: Academic Press.

Side Effects of Medical Treatments and Settings

Kornfield, D. S. (1977). The hospital environment: Its impact on the patient. In R. H. Moos (Ed.), *Coping with Physical Illness*. New York: Plenum.

Redd, W. H., & Andrykowski, M. A. (1982). Behavioral interventions in cancer treatment: Controlling aversive reactions to chemotherapy. *Journal of Consulting and Clinical Psychology, 50*(6), 1018–1030.

Pain Management

Blanchard, E. B., & Andrasik, F. (1985). *Management of chronic headaches*. New York: Pergamon Press.

Holzman, A. D., & Turk, D. C. (1986). *Pain management: A handbook of psychological treatment approaches*. New York: Pergamon Press.

Compliance with Treatment Regimens

Haynes, R. B., Taylor, D. W., & Sackett, D. L. (1979). *Compliance in health care*. Baltimore: The Johns Hopkins University Press.

Masur III, F. T. (1981). Adherence to health care regimens. In C. K. Prokop & L. A. Bradley (Eds.), *Medical Psychology: Contributions to Behavioral Medicine*. New York: Academic Press.

Coping with Chronic Illness

Burish, T. G., & Bradley, L. A. (Eds.). (1983). *Coping with chronic disease*. New York: Academic.

Moos, R. H. (Ed.). (1977). *Coping with physical illness*. New York: Plenum.

Death and Dying

Levy, S. (1983). The process of death and dying. In T. G. Burish & L. A. Bradley (Eds.), *Coping with chronic disease*. New York: Academic Press.

Worden, J. W. (1982). *Grief counseling and grief therapy*. New York: Springer.

Rehabilitation

Brucker, B. S. (1983). Spinal cord injuries. In T. G. Burish & L. A. Bradley (Eds.), *Coping with chronic disease*. New York: Academic Press.

Gordon, W. A., & Diller, L. (1983). Stroke: Coping with a cognitive deficit. In T. G. Burish & L. A. Bradley (Eds.), *Coping with chronic disease*. New York: Academic.

Prevention and Behavioral Health

Matarazzo, J. D., Weiss, S. M., Herd, J. A., Miller, N. E., & Weiss, S. M. (Eds.). (1984). *Behavioral Health: A handbook of health enhancement and disease prevention*. New York: Wiley.

Psychophysiological Self-Regulation

Nerenz, D. R., & Leventhal, H. (1983). Self-regulation theory in chronic illness. In T. G. Burish & L. A. Bradley (Eds.), *Coping with chronic disease*. New York: Academic.

Olton, D. S., & Noonberg, A. R. (1980). *Biofeedback: Clinical applications in behavioral medicine*. Englewood Cliffs, NJ: Prentice-Hall.

Health Care Systems and Health Providers

Hay, D., & Oken, D. (1977). The psychological stresses of intensive care unit nursing. In R. H. Moos (Ed.), *Coping with physical illness*. New York: Plenum.

Maslach, C. (1982). *Burnout: The cost of caring*. Englewood Cliffs, NJ: Prentice-Hall.

Stone, G. C. (1979). Psychology in the health system. In G. C. Stone, F. Cohen, & N. E. Adler (Eds.), *Health psychology: A handbook*. San Francisco: Jossey-Bass.

Chapter 8
Special Issues in Assessment and Intervention

Previous chapters have presented frameworks with which to conduct a thorough psychological assessment and to develop intervention strategies. This chapter will shift focus from the content and methods of assessment and intervention to the barriers and problems encountered while working in the field of clinical health psychology, with suggestions for solutions where possible. Discussion will focus on practical concerns relevant to both inpatient and outpatient settings. Case examples, carefully chosen to reflect pertinent practice topics, represent actual experiences that the authors have either encountered or witnessed.

CLARIFYING THE REFERRAL QUESTION

It is not uncommon to receive vague, poorly defined assessment questions. In our experience, we have found that many physicians and other referral sources are still unclear as to what services clinical health psychologists provide and what kinds of information are helpful when making a consultation request. As a result, assessment questions are often ambiguous, unclear, too specific, untimely, or inappropriate. Listed next are some common problems with written referrals.

Determining the Reason for the Referral

"Patient recently diagnosed as having cervical cancer, refuses surgery." Given the limited amount of information, it is not clear as to what services are being requested. One could guess that the referring doctor or nurse is frustrated by the patient's refusal of a surgical procedure and wants the psychologist to convince the patient otherwise. In

111

this type of case, it is essential that the clinical health psychologist attempt to garner additional information from a variety of sources, especially the consultee, prior to actually talking with the patient. Additionally, the psychologist should be aware that this consultation might reflect conflict between the value systems of the patient and the health care system. Assessment needs to be directed toward both the patient and the staff.

Handling Predetermined Procedures

"Patient is very tense and has migraine headaches. Please give biofeedback." In this example, the referral source is prescribing a type of treatment that might or might not be appropriate or cost-effective for the patient. We have found this to be a frequent problem when a referral source is personally invested in a particular technique. When a specific form of treatment (e.g., biofeedback) has already been prescribed for the patient by another professional, problems are created for the consultant. First, patients expect the prescribed treatment to be delivered, and the fact that such a treatment might be inappropriate must be addressed explicitly. In doing this, it is important to remember that patients could feel they are getting "something less" if they do not receive the "promised" form of treatment. Further, in an attempt to ally with the current provider, the patient might "split" loyalties between the referral source and the psychologist. This can enhance the gulf between professionals and result in fragmented care. Thus, a clear rationale for not providing the treatment should be given along with the alternative treatment plan. Referral sources also occasionally order specific tests, such as the MMPI, that are not the appropriate assessment techniques for the domain in question (e.g., ability to comprehend complicated medical regimen).

As well as dealing with patient issues, when inappropriate procedures are ordered, the clinical health psychologist must communicate the inappropriateness of "prescription" consultations to the referral source. In our opinion, the best way to avert further conflict in this regard is to speak cordially, but directly, with the referral source and to clarify what represents an appropriate referral and what does not. Often physicians and medical personnel are so accustomed to ordering specific tests and procedures that they are unaware that the same process does not apply between disciplines. Alternatively, it has also been found that physicians prescribe treatments such as biofeedback or stress management as a shorthand method of asking for assessment and intervention with general psychological problems. Many believe that their patients are more receptive to this language on the referral form.

It is important to train referral sources as to how to discuss the referral with their patients. For example, one can ask the physician to help make the clinician's job easier by preparing the patient for the referral, or one can suggest that careful preparation might avoid having the patient become angry at the physician. We suggest that a physician explicitly state that the referral is not being made because he or she thinks it's "all in the patient's head," but because of his or her interest in the whole patient and awareness that other disciplines have certain skills to offer that have been helpful in similar cases. Physicians need to emphasize that *all* illnesses have psychological components and thus are in the head, because mind and body cannot be separated.

Identifying the Patient

The identified patient might not be the target for intervention. Consider this referral request, "Patient is a 17-year-old female student undergoing bone marrow transplant. Patient acting inappropriately on ward by refusing to acknowledge depression." After the clinical health psychologist interviewed this patient, it was apparent that the patient had a clear understanding of her medical condition and possible consequences. Her religious beliefs, general optimistic style, and strong social relations were interacting in a manner that produced effective coping techniques and a minimum of psychological distress or depression. This example demonstrates a case in which medical personnel had projected their own fears and emotions onto the patient. Consequently, when the patient did not behave in the expected manner, a consultation was generated. In this example, the patient was actually coping with the illness better than the staff. As a result, the clinical health psychologist needed to refocus attention to acknowledge staff concerns and stressors as the potential targets for intervention. Although it is not always efficacious to attempt explanation of psychological defenses (projection), recognition of staff concerns, and education regarding individual differences, can help alleviate some of their anxieties when a patient does not behave in the typical fashion.

Sometimes the referral comes about because of family reactions to the patient or the illness. One referral we received concerned adjustment issues after loss of sight in a 40-year-old man. Upon further exploration with both the referral source and the patient, it was determined that the wife's reaction to this loss was the real reason for referral and thus the more appropriate target of intervention.

Another problem in "identifying the patient" can result from problems the physician is experiencing. Having personal knowledge of the referral source can alleviate some of the problems encountered in consultation requests. We once received a consultation request for evaluation of "somatic symptoms caused by stress" in a patient with a documented goiter condition. The initial evaluation with this patient revealed no significant psychological problems. A repeat evaluation was scheduled, including another interview and an MMPI. Again, there was insufficient evidence of psychological problems to warrant speculation about psychological factors as etiologic in the patient's condition. However, several colleagues, who were knowledgeable about the referring physician, believed that she herself was suffering from rather major psychological concerns and was likely to misperceive patients. Direct feedback to the physician concerning lack of significant psychopathology in the patient was provided in a nonthreatening, supportive manner. As the discussion progressed, the physician disclosed that she might have distorted information about the patient.

Dealing with Choice of Inappropriate Provider

"Patient is 49-year-old single, male who has undergone bypass surgery. Unable to care for self at home during recovery. Please arrange for supportive services." Discussion revealed the confusion that sometimes results from many services being offered within an inpatient setting. In this case, the referring resident wanted the patient to receive home nursing care during the early stages of recovery. The referral source in this case contacted the inappropriate provider (psychologist) for a type of intervention desired (social work). Division of labor is not always clear among the disciplines of psychiatry, psychology, and social work, which are sometimes housed in separate departments. In fact, these departments often overlap in services provided, thereby justifying the resulting confusion. If the clinician is working within a teaching hospital, one can expect an especially high incidence of this type of error during times of medical resident rotations and arrival of new residents (July 1 of each year).

Self-referred outpatients, and, occasionally, physician-referred patients can also be mistaken about the types of services provided by a clinical health psychologist. Much of the public remains poorly informed regarding the traditional differences between psychiatry and psychology. When a profession becomes even more specialized within a given discipline (i.e., clinical health psychology versus clinical psychology), it is not surprising that people are perplexed when certain services are not offered.

> Mrs. M. was a 35-year-old, married, Caucasian female with a chronic history of severe migraine headaches. She was referred by her neurologist to an outpatient headache management program for evaluation and treatment. Upon completion of the initial interview, it became obvious that the patient expected the clinical health psychologist to offer some form of medication treatment, and expressed considerable dismay and agitation when this type of "headache management" was not available.

DEALING WITH POORLY TIMED
REFERRAL REQUESTS

Occasionally, the timing of a consultation request is inappropriate. Referrals can be premature or extensively delayed. We have received more than one consultation request asking for evaluation of a patient's mental status within 6 hours of a motor vehicle accident. In these instances, when the consultant arrived at bedside, he found the patients in a comatose state, clearly unable to meet the demands of the assessment process. In this situation it is best to respond to the physician's concerns but also to explain the limits of the psychological assessment process. Scheduling follow-up times and coordinating those with the referral source will assure him or her that the request is not being ignored.

Alternatively, we have also discovered that well-meaning health care providers have delayed a consultation request for psychological evaluation or treatment beyond the point of a consultant's ability to provide optimal services. This is particularly true when the referral source has attempted to deal with the patient's problems herself or himself, without seeking a psychologist's opinion. As a result, by the time the clinical health psychologist is consulted, she or he often finds a much more severe problem than had initially occurred. As an example, consider the following case:

> Mr. S. was a 54-year-old, Caucasian male of Italian descent. He was hospitalized for lower extremity edema and phlebitis in his left leg. Upon admission to the unit, the patient behaved in a very arrogant, noncompliant, and demanding manner (did not stay in bed with leg elevated), which intimidated the newly arrived medical residents. Mr. S. adamantly denied noncompliance with medical regimen; however, laboratory results suggested that he had not been taking the prescribed medication as required. As Mr. S.'s hospitalization progressed, he became increasingly disruptive. The medical team attempted to independently deal with his behaviors by "bullying" him. As a result, the patient became even more agitated and began acting toward medical personnel in a belligerent manner. The psychology service was then consulted.

Upon arriving at bedside, the psychologist conducted an individual interview with the patient that assessed previous history of adherence to medical regimens, general psychological condition, and reinforcers for noncompliance. It was revealed that this patient was suffering from a bipolar affective disorder, manic phase, in addition to having long-standing personality problems that included narcissistic features. Given these psychological parameters, it became increasingly clear that this patient would be unlikely to adhere to any complicated medication regimen (he was also noncompliant with psychotropic medication), especially when feeling pressured by staff. Had the clinical health psychologist been consulted earlier, staff members could have been provided with information to help them reframe the situation and with explicit instructions on case management.

DUMPING AND TURFING

Dumping and *turfing* are two terms with which the clinical health psychologist will unfortunately become familiar. These terms represent assessment and intervention requests for patients that other professionals no longer wish to be responsible for. As such, the patients are dumped or turfed to a different department or service. Occasionally patients are referred for psychological assessment because of the physician's inability to determine a medical diagnosis. It is often unfortunately assumed that, if the patient is not physically ill and still complains, the patient *must* be psychologically ill. This is especially true in cases where patients have a previous history of psychological problems.

Medical personnel are not the only professionals to turf patients. In psychological and psychiatric practices, patients who present with frequent and multiple medical complaints are often viewed as less desirable clients or "not amenable to psychotherapy," and are thus referred for "stress management." This type of referral implies that the consultant is differentiating stress management from psychotherapy, reserving the latter term for those treatment approaches that are perceived as more insight-oriented in nature (and usually viewed as having higher status in the field). Consequently, outpatients who present with somatization issues and who are not YAVIS (young, attractive, verbal, intelligent, and successful) might be referred to a clinical health psychologist for no clinically sound reason. That is, because the primary therapist has no professional interest in dealing with this kind of patient problem, he or she turfs the patient to the clinical health psychologist. In this case, the psychologist should again communicate back to the referral source if the consultation is inappropriate, stating clearly the reasons for that determination. However, often the clinical health psychologist has services useful to these patients, whereas more traditional ones have failed.

PROBLEMS IN OBTAINING
BACKGROUND INFORMATION

Throughout this guidebook we have described key sources that offer background information on the patient and his or her illness. In the actual course of uncovering information, the clinical health psychologist is likely to encounter several roadblocks. Ultimately, the amount of time and energy channeled into pursuing background information will be based on the clinician's judgment concerning the necessity and utility of the sought-after information. Difficulties in gathering background information include inability to understand medical terminology, inability to obtain release of information, unavailability of records, and poor handwriting.

Lack of Medical Expertise

Although the clinical health psychologist will have studied basic medical terminology and will have a general understanding of common medical disorders, many technical reports focus solely on the medical aspects of disease and do not address psychological ramifications of the illness. Consequently, the clinical health psychologist is often left with a technical, biochemical report that incompletely meets the demands of a biopsychosocial perspective. We have found it extremely helpful to ask our medical colleagues to explain various aspects of specific diseases, and their implications, in terms that are understandable to nonmedical professionals. It has been our experience that most physicians are not only willing to provide this information but also respect our judgment and efforts in attempting to understand these issues.

Inability to Obtain Releases of Information

Patients might be unable or unwilling to release information concerning previous psychological or medical treatments. It is not uncommon for patients to forget, or to be too ill to recall, the names of previous health care providers. This is especially true when they have been in treatment with multiple providers over the course of many years. Alternatively, some patients prefer not to disclose information concerning past treatments, as they fear it could be perceived in a negative manner or be damaging to them in some way. Inability to obtain releases of information also limits with whom the clinician can speak. That is, except under extreme or urgent circumstances, it is unethical to speak with family members, friends, previous treatment providers, or employers regarding the patient without first having the patient's consent to do so. If the patient is not willing to provide releases of information, the therapist needs to decide the possible ramifications on treatment and to determine whether or not to proceed under these circumstances.

Unavailability of Records

Assuming that a release of information has been provided, the clinician will quickly discover that medical and psychological records are not easily obtainable. Records are occasionally lost or unavailable at time of assessment. Particularly in an outpatient setting, the clinical health psychologist might need to be more persistent in obtaining previous treatment histories from a variety of sources and to continue the process of gathering information throughout the first few sessions. Further, records obtained from private sources are typically summaries of the patient's treatment. As a result, such things as a complete history of physical complaints, number of visits, previous medications, and subjective impressions might not be reflected in the records. It could be wise to communicate via telephone with relevant private practitioners to insure thorough understanding of the patient and his or her illness.

Poor Handwriting

Jokingly, the sine qua non of a good physician has been the degree of impairment of his or her handwriting. In actual practice, poor handwriting is no laughing matter. Review of medical records is unavoidably hampered by the inability to read medical personnel's description, diagnosis, or treatment of the patient. Not only is poor handwriting frustrating to read, but it can also lead to misdiagnosis or mismanagement of the patient. From our perspective, one is only as effective as one's ability to communicate.

Failure to Gather Background Information

Consider the following example:

Dr. Young was a fourth-year psychiatric resident completing his training in a general medical hospital. He received a consultation to assess depression on a patient who had undergone surgery for cancer. When Dr. Young arrived on the ward, the patient's medical records were being used by another service provider. In his rush to complete this evaluation and attend to other patients, Dr. Young conducted an interview with the patient without reviewing the records or talking with medical personnel, making the assumption that this patient was probably suffering from an adjustment reaction to the surgery. During the interview, the patient did not speak with Dr. Young and frequently stared off into space, apparently ignoring the resident's questions. The physician concluded in his report that the patient was severely depressed and exhibiting signs of catatonia.

Unfortunately for Dr. Young, he later learned that the patient was almost completely deaf and unable to comprehend any of his interview questions. The gathering of background information could be the first thing to be ignored by the rushed and time-pressured clinician. However, it is an important aspect of accurate evaluation and treatment. Also, recent malpractice litigation suggests one might be responsible for being aware of a patient's past record (*Jablonski v. United States*, 1983).

INITIAL CONTACT WITH
THE PATIENT

Working Hypotheses

The clinical health psychologist's immediate task in formulating working hypotheses could be easier within an inpatient setting than an outpatient setting because of the availability of records in-house. In any case, it is crucial that the clinician be knowledgeable about the nature of the medical problem and relevant treatments *prior* to seeing the patient. For example, it would be useless to interview a candidate for penile prosthesis surgery (in which it is critical to assess how realistic the patient's expectations are) without being aware of the probable outcomes of this type of surgery. The clinician also needs to know the potential psychological concomitants of the patient's physiological symptoms and pharmacological therapies prior to interviewing the patient.

In addition to considering possible interactions among the person, the disorder, and the treatment plan, the consultant should have an understanding of the patient's preparedness, if any, for a psychological consultation. Before actually making initial contact with the patient, the clinical health psychologist should be prepared to answer several questions:

1. Does the patient know that a psychologist has been consulted?
2. What might a psychological consultation mean to the patient?
3. Given background information obtained, what is the best way to approach this particular person?

The first question addresses a very common problem. Physicians frequently request a psychological evaluation without advising the patient. Bagheri and colleagues (Bagheri, Lane, Kline, & Araujo, 1981) stated that 68% of patients within a medical center had not been informed by their physicians that a psychiatric consultation had been requested. The primary reason for not advising patients of the referral was a fear that the patient might see the consultation as an insult. Other common reasons were that the physician did not think of it, the physician was too busy, the physician thought the patient might become belligerent or refuse consultation, and the physician feared that the patient might lose faith in him or her.

It is always important to deal with the reason for referral at the beginning of the interview. A good opening question can be to ask the patient about her or his understanding of the reason for the referral. A problem frequently uncovered is that the physician has indicated to the patient that he or she has "nothing further to offer medically." This, especially when associated with referral to a psychologist, is then interpreted by the patient as meaning that the problem is "in my head." On numerous occasions, this is not what the referral source meant (e.g., the patient might have documented medical problems accounting for the symptoms reported). Because patients themselves often ascribe to mind–body dualism, they frequently misinterpret physicians.

The third question serves as a reminder that each patient is unique, with her or his own idiosyncratic expectations, fears, coping mechanisms, abilities, and medical problems. Patients should not become a "label" or a "diagnosis."

Problems with Settings

With today's soaring costs of medical care, many facilities have eliminated the private patient room. As a result, the patient's privacy is often quite limited, and the clinician needs to be acutely aware of confidentiality issues. If the patient is feeling well enough, and there are no medical contraindications, it might be possible to request to meet the person in the clinician's office. However, this is generally not the case, particularly for the initial contact. Therefore, the psychologist might need to make necessary adjustments in his or her own interview style or make other necessary arrangements to insure confidentiality. The persistent clinician might be able to locate a family, conference, or waiting room that is not in use. Generally, if such rooms are available, there is little objection to allowing the psychologist access. Unfortunately, many patients are not ambulatory and require bedrest, thereby eliminating the possibility of complete privacy. When the interview must take place in a semiprivate room, the clinician should, at a minimum, close the curtain around the patient's bed and talk in a lowered voice. It is also sometimes possible to request that the other patient leave temporarily. In our experience, roommates are usually agreeable to this need for privacy.

Problems with Scheduling the Patient

Although scheduling the patient for an initial evaluation session seems like a simple task, it can prove to be very difficult. Working in a hospital poses several problems that the outpatient psychologist might not have to face. Medical procedures take precedence over all other procedures. As a result, patients are frequently off the ward for laboratory work and treatment. Scheduling an appointment with the patient through either the ward clerk or the charge nurse can alleviate this difficulty. However, the clinical health psychologist needs to have sufficient flexibility in her or his schedule to allow for variation in hours.

Scheduling the medical outpatient poses the same difficulties as scheduling any psychological outpatient, with a few additional considerations. Depending on the patient's health status and stamina, it might be better to schedule a shorter appointment (in duration) than is customary. Physical limitations of patients also often necessitate special considerations in parking arrangements, wheelchair access, and restroom facilities. Additionally, many medical patients prefer appointments in the morning or the afternoon, secondary to medication regimens and other treatment (radiation, OT, PT) or because of personal preference (ability to arrange transportation, disrupted sleep schedules or work schedules). If the clinical health psychologist can remain flexible in scheduling patients, he or she will be more able to capitalize on the optimum performance of the patient.

A common problem in outpatient settings is a lack of follow-through by the patient in scheduling an appointment after referral. One means of overcoming this problem is for the clinical health psychologist to contact the patient initially, not waiting for the patient to call. Alternatively, the clinician can train the referral source to make "strong" referrals. Provision to patients of business cards and written materials, describing services and location, is also useful. Depending upon the nature of the outpatient service, it is often desirable for the clinical health psychologist to schedule patient appointments in the outpatient medical clinic in conjunction with other medical visits.

The Reluctant or Hostile Patient

Clinical health psychologists, probably more so than those in traditional practice, must deal with reluctant or hostile patients in the initial visit. The reasons for this can be numerous, but we have found four common ones: (a) The patient was not told about the referral to a psychologist; (b) The patient has negative perceptions about psychological intervention for what the patient, and perhaps the physician, has defined as a medical problem (as indicated, most patients are mind–body dualists also); (c) The patient is being asked to shift from a biomedical model of understanding disease (with its passive, external locus of control) to a biopsychosocial model of understanding disease, with different responsibilities and a more internal locus of control; and (d) Patients are rarely self-referred to a clinical health psychologist and thus tend to be more skeptical about the initial session that those patients who have self-initiated contact with a psychologist. Of these, the most typical source of reluctance is patients' focus on the medical aspects of the problem and anger about their doctors' implying it "might all be in your head."

As mentioned earlier, it is important to gauge a patient's reaction and emotional state relative to the referral for psychological evaluation. If this is not done adequately, with appropriate adjustment in interviewing style, the assessment can yield invalid data, the patient might not commit to any type of treatment, and the patient might sabotage treatment attempts.

We and others (see DeGood, 1983; Weisman, 1978) have observed several early warning signs of patient reluctance or hostility related to psychological assessment, including

1. Refusal to schedule an appointment or to show up for return visits.
2. Anger and bewilderment in the initial session as to why the referral was made or being closed-mouthed in discussing his or her problem.
3. Interest in the initial session, then "yes, but-ing" and taking personal exception to what has been discussed.
4. Statements implying that the patient wishes to pursue other medical treatments first.

The clinical health psychologist must be alert to these cues, because he or she has the challenging task of establishing rapport in a relatively short time. We find DeGood's (1983) and Weisman's (1978) suggestions of ways to facilitate reduction of patient reluctance and hostility toward psychological intervention very helpful:

1. *Try to establish rapport with the patient.* Self-introduction of name and position is of course required. Establish eye contact with the patient. When possible, sit down while talking with the patient. By not towering over an individual who might already feel inferior because of role issues, you are likely to make the person feel less threatened. Ask the patient what she or he understands was the reason for the referral.

2. *Avoid asking yes–no questions.* Yes–No questions are usually not questions but statements in disguise. The reluctant patient quickly assumes that the assessing psychologist has already determined a diagnosis without listening to his or her comments or questions.

3. *Defuse the organic-versus-functional myth.* Depending on how the primary physician made the referral, this can be more or less of a problem. It can be useful to simply state overtly that many patients have concerns about referral to a psychologist for medical problems. Further discussion should include the patient's feelings and thoughts about this and some mention of the interaction between physical illness and psychological state. Allow the patient to present physical symptoms for a short time. Acknowledging the real aspects of the medical condition is helpful and reduces patient anxiety.

4. *Avoid "psychologizing" the patient's symptoms.* Many patients referred to a clinical health psychologist are not psychologically minded and are

not interested in insight. It is important to meet some of the needs of the patient and "give" her or him something concrete in the first interview. This could entail some explanation of psychophysiological aspects of the medical problem, a rationale for treatment, and perhaps some diary forms for self-monitoring of symptoms.

5. *Shape adequate beliefs rather than challenge misconceptions.* The initial contact should involve mostly listening and encouragement. Challenging the patient's reluctance to participate will probably result in the patient's passively-aggressively not returning. We find it useful to use the technique of Kleinman et al. (1977) of eliciting and negotiating the patient's illness-belief model. Table 8.1 illustrates with a miniscript an appropriate means of treatment presentation.

6. *Present treatment strategy in a positive fashion, rather than as a last resort.* Often, patient referral to the clinical health psychologist is done as a last resort after traditional medical management has failed. Distressed patients unfortunately perceive this communication from the physician as "you have failed" and are thus being "relegated to psychology." Providing a clear rationale and explanation of treatment can help increase motivation and compliance.

7. *Foster realistic expectations about treatment.* The patient generally does not understand the process or time commitment required in psychological treatment. Providing the patient with an outline of how psychological treatment differs from medical treatment is important. Issues of special importance include the facts that there is no sudden cure, the patient will be more of an active participant than perhaps in previous medical treatments, and there will be ups and downs in the course of treatment. Such a discussion can prevent premature therapy termination due to unmet expectations and to frustration.

8. *Clarify other treatment roles.* The patient will want to know how the psychological treatment will interface with his or her ongoing medical management. The clinical health psychologist must be familiar with other treatments and be able to provide a clear explanation of how the various treatment procedures will interact. Be sure the patient understands that this is not an either–or situation.

The psychologist must be vigilant to the overt or covert presentation of concerns by the patient and must facilitate open discussion to dispel myths and to reassure the patient that her or his concerns are not unusual. The task is not to *coerce* the patient into obtaining the service but to dispel misconceptions that prove to be barriers to obtaining help. Protection of the patient's right to consent is paramount, except when contraindicated by law.

Table 8.1. Sample Script of Patient Interview

Interviewer: Mr. Jones, what is your understanding about why you are here to see me today?

Patient: Well my doctor, he told me to come here.

Interviewer: Why do you think he suggested that?

Patient: I don't know. I guess he thinks it would help, but I don't see how, not unless you can give me something that will help with this pain in my back. That's the only thing that's bothering me.

Interviewer: Well I'm not sure what we have at this point that might be helpful for your pain. That's what we'll try to find out. But I was wondering if you had any thoughts about why you're here to see a psychologist?

Patient: No, my doctor told me to come.

Interviewer: Well, sometimes patients think that they get sent to see me because their doctor doesn't believe that their pain is real. Have you ever felt that way?

Patient: Well I should know. I feel my pain, I know it's real.

Interviewer: Well of course it is, and you're right—you are the only one who can feel it. No doctor can. Which I guess might feel a bit lonely sometimes, if it seems no one else can feel what you feel.

Patient: Well that's true. You know they've done all these tests, and they can't find anything wrong.

Interviewer: What do you mean by wrong?

Patient: Well they can't operate. They say it would just make my back worse.

Interviewer: So maybe what your doctor meant was that he didn't have any medical treatments that might be useful.

Patient: Yes, that's right. I guess I'm a lost cause. But I think I'm managing as best I can. I mean I'm not ready for the nuthouse yet.

Interviewer: Well people don't get sent to me because they're ready for the nuthouse. I get to see patients just like you because their doctors understand that there have been developments in the field of psychology that have sometimes been useful to patients with chronic pain problems.

Patient: Oh come on, you mean that I could just talk myself out of this pain?

Interviewer: Well I'm not sure, but it might be possible for you to learn to live with it without suffering so much. Learning is sometimes a big part of pain and coping with pain, you know.

Patient: Now I didn't learn this pain. I hurt my back at work lifting a sack of cement.

Interviewer: Of course, and you know we can't do anything about that original injury. But you know its very normal for a pain that has been going on for a while to get affected by other things. You know bodily processes can be conditioned. Let me give you an example. If I hold up a bright lemon in front of you, now imagine this in my hand here, and then I cut it with a knife so that you can see the juicy pulp inside. And then I hold it here and begin to squeeze. Now imagine those drops running down and the squishing sound it makes as I squeeze the lemon tight. By the way do you feel anything in your mouth? Sometimes people do, they actually feel saliva forming under their tongues. And that is *real*, not imaginary, although of course it was a learned response. I mean you never really felt the lemon itself.

Patient: Yeah, I felt that. So how does this relate to may pain? My pain is caused by that squished disc I have, not some lemon.

Continued

Table 8.1. *Continued*

Interviewer: Well, I think of pain as a big pie we can divide into pieces. Some of those pieces we might actually be able to take out, like pieces of your pain that could be due to not managing your activity level well, or due to having been conditioned—affected by learning. And some pieces could be affected by your mood. We all know that if we have the flu after a bad day at work we feel a lot worse than if we have the flu and it's been a good day. And you can't have pain without it having affected your life in some way. How has it affected yours?

Patient: Well I have been more depressed—and my family is about fed up with me—you know they don't understand—I think they think I'm faking this sometimes, but I know I hurt.

Interviewer: Yes you do, now tell me more about it. . . .

Other Considerations in Interviewing

It is often the case that the psychologist is the first professional to really listen to what the patient has to report; hence, he or she might obtain more information than previous health care professionals. The patient might relish the opportunity to tell her or his story by detailing specific events leading up to the referral. Given the chance, patients sometimes tell the psychologist details that had either escaped their memory in the time-pressured discussions with their physicians or were withheld in the absence of sufficient rapport, especially if the information did not appear relevant to the patient. We had one patient reveal for the first time that she had never been adequately treated for a past episode of syphilis because she assumed her physician would no longer care for her if he knew of this disease. It is important to document symptoms when appropriate, so that information becomes available to other health care providers.

BOUNDARY ISSUES IN CLINICAL HEALTH PSYCHOLOGY

When working with medical–surgical patients, the clinical health psychologist is likely to encounter special "boundary" issues that are not as salient in traditional outpatient services. Clinical health psychologists could find themselves involved in a variety of behaviors that are not part of traditional therapeutic practice (e.g. helping a patient rotate in bed, assisting a patient with various prostheses, or closing a tracheotomy so that the patient can speak). As a result, more traditionally trained clinicians might need to make adjustments in their professional identities in order to become health care providers in clinical health psychology. One must become at ease interacting with patients with various needs. It can be useful and acceptable to patients to ask them how you can best help them in facilitating an interview.

Nudity

It is not uncommon within inpatient settings for the clinician to encounter patients in various states of undress. For example, as part of a multidisciplinary team, one of the authors regularly attended patient rounds on a coronary care unit. During these rounds, patients were physically examined in the usual manner, which necessitated partial nudity. As a result, the psychologist initially wrestled with professional identity issues and felt that her presence was intrusive on the patient's rights. Identifying and processing differing practice standards for different settings and reframing her professional interests as *health care*, rather than *therapy*, alleviated this initial discomfort.

Touching

In the practice of clinical health psychology, therapists often touch their patients in the course of their work. As an example, touching patients always occurs in applying biofeedback electrodes and is part of standard practice. Other forms of touching include gently holding a patient's hand to offer reassurance, helping a patient in and out of bed, or assisting a patient with walking. These acts of touching differ dramatically from traditionally established taboos and can cause a certain amount of anxiety for the psychologist.

SPECIAL ISSUES IN ASSESSMENT

As detailed in chapters 4 and 5, professional concerns regarding the use of psychometric assessment devices and evaluation procedures include lack of normative data on medical–surgical patients, misuse of psychological data by nonpsychological personnel, and applicability of standard interpretive rules. In addition to those concerns, there are several practical issues the clinician faces. Even when good normative data for medical–surgical patients are available, the answers to many diagnostic and treatment questions are not easily answered with available tests. That is, psychological assessment techniques typically do not yield "clean" interpretations of a patient's problem. Our inability, as a profession, to specifically state that the problem is one thing or another is often quite frustrating to a physician who is hoping to establish some "concrete" diagnosis. The clinical health psychologist needs to feel comfortable furnishing sometimes ambiguous test results, and not feel pressured to "go beyond the data" to satisfy an implied demand to solve a problem.

Neglecting the Impact of Environment

Put yourself in the following situation:

Two days ago, you had a mild heart attack. As a result, you had to end all work responsibilities and are now lying in a bed in the intensive care unit (ICU). There are no clocks, calendars, or windows in your room. You are dressed in a hospital gown, confined to bed, and required to use a bedpan. A nurse observes you through a window, and another nurse checks your vital signs every hour, without telling you the results of those tests. There is an intravenous tube in your arm, but you are not aware of its purpose. You have never been hospitalized before and are unsure as to how to behave. The doctor has not been by to see you today, and you are unsure as to the extent of damage to your heart. You have also been given a mild narcotic to help you rest but have not been told of potential side effects. Your family, also being unfamiliar with the situation, is acting in an anxious manner. Relatives who live away from your city have been notified of your heart attack. A clinical health psychologist then enters your room, introduces himself, and advises you that your physician has requested an evaluation for depressed mood.

In interpreting data obtained from patients, we have repeatedly mentioned the importance of considering the impact of the immediate setting. In the example just given, the psychologist must take into consideration the effect of environmental ICU and situational events (e.g., new role as patient, unfamiliarity with hospitals) when assessing potential causes of depressed mood. According to attribution theory, observers, particularly clinicians, due to their person-focused training (Jones & Nisbett, 1971), overestimate the role of dispositional (trait) factors when inferring causes of behavior. As a safeguard, then, the clinical health psychologist should pay particular attention to environmental cues that could precipitate maladaptive behavior. Failure to do so will result in erroneous conclusions about the causality and permanence of the patient's condition.

Underestimating Psychopathology

Clinical health psychologists sometimes underestimate the impact of psychopathology and its relationship to the medical–surgical problem. The clinical health psychologist must have as strong a background in psychopathology as any clinical psychologist. Although obviously not all medical–surgical patients are disturbed, a National Institute of Mental Health study suggested that 20% of American adults do suffer from psychiatric disorders (Leo, 1984). Thus, it is very likely that the clinical health psychologist will have to deal with psychopathology. Indeed, up to 20% to 25% of medical–surgical inpatients have been diagnosed as suffering from depression severe enough to warrant treatment (Shevitz et al., 1976); thus the clinician must be skilled in this area.

Remaining Open to Alternatives

Clinical health psychologists should abide by the following well-known saying: "Stay open-minded, but not so open that your brains fall out." Sometimes rather nontraditional types of assessment and intervention are suggested, as highly novel approaches might be required. For example, when attempting to assess a patient for possible self-infection of an open wound (Munchausen's syndrome), one strategy used was to tape the patient's hands (with consent), to determine if the infection would then clear up. In another case, spot fingernail cultures were ordered in order to arrive at a more definitive assessment of the source and means of infection. Another example of creative intervention is illustrated by the clinician who suggested to a patient facing laryngectomy (and who had a booming baritone voice, which he used regularly in a barbershop quartet) that he tape various messages to his family as a means of preserving his voice (much like a family photo). Thus, his young grandchildren would have a record of what he had sounded like prior to surgery.

Coping with Competing Agendas

In providing clinical services, the psychologist might have to deal with competing agendas with respect to a particular case and be quite clear as to *who* is the client. For example, in one presurgical screening of a kidney donor, we became very much aware of the surgeon's desire for a "clean bill of psychological health" so that the kidney could be obtained for his own patient. (This was the physician's third consultation in an effort to psychologically "clear" the donor for surgery.) The potential donor was also extremely eager to undergo the operation, as it gave him the opportunity to "atone for past sins" within the family. The hospital's agenda was for written confirmation that there was no psychological risk associated with the donation. Given the nature of the case, none of these parties was satisfied with the results and recommendations of the psychological evaluation, which indicated that although the potential donor demonstrated a clear understanding of the procedure, he also had a long history of poor impulse control and instances in which he manifested poor judgment in decisions related to self-care. The report could not give the patient a "clean bill." Nevertheless, the donation did occur after the patient obtained a court judgment, which satisfied the hospital's malpractice lawyers, that he was not *legally* incompetent to make this decision.

Coping with the Hostile Physician

As in any profession, there are hostile and arrogant physicians. Strategies for coping include a task-oriented focus on the patient's needs as a mutual goal, consistent assertiveness, confrontation as necessary, and a wealth of good humor. If the goal is to change physician behavior toward the patient, emphasizing benefits that would accrue to the physician is critical to laying the groundwork for change.

SPECIAL CONSIDERATIONS IN TREATMENT

Determining an Adequate Trial

It is important for the clinical health psychologist to understand what constitutes an adequate trial of treatment for any given approach, as there are significant ethical problems with persisting in an ineffective treatment regimen. In making this decision, the clinician should consider both patient variables (such as motivation, attendance, consistency, and acceptance of the biopsychosocial model) and treatment variables (what procedures have been attempted, what revisions in protocol have occurred in response to lack of change, what the limitations of the strategy are.

Understanding the nature of previous treatment attempts and reasons for failure can also help the clinician decide when to pursue other forms of intervention or when to cease treatment. We cannot underscore enough the need to obtain numerous details about previous treatments. When closely scrutinized, the relaxation therapy or biofeedback treatment previously obtained can have been very inadequate in terms of design and implementation.

In the therapist's zeal to help patients learn to cope with various medical and psychological problems, he or she should not lose sight of the fact that not all problems are treatable, at least by methods currently available. The experienced clinician will accept the limitations of interventions, thereby avoiding a failure experience for both the patient and herself or himself.

Keeping the Therapeutic Contract Clear

Medical–surgical patients can be in multiple psychological treatments. This is particularly true when a patient has been referred by another mental health professional for an adjunctive intervention for a problem such as headache. Patients often begin relating personal material that is more appropriate to the other therapy. It is necessary for the clinical health psychologist to contain these statements and focus treatment on the identified problem. Alternatively, the therapist might need to renegotiate the existing contract with both patient and referral source.

Interrupting Psychological Treatment

Treatment interruptions can occur due to either planned or unplanned circumstances. It is not uncommon for patients to take a hiatus from psychological treatment while attending to acute medical problems. Patients also request interruption of treatment for financial reasons (insurance benefits do not adequately pay for psychological services) or for personal reasons.

A common reason for treatment interruption has to do with premature discharge, which can occur, from the psychologist's point of view, for a variety of reasons. Administrative pressures to adhere to DRGs is increasing in medical practice. As a result, physicians could discharge their patients as soon as they are medically cleared, not considering psychological intervention as a reasonable cause for extending hospitalization. Consequently, the clinician might begin an intervention procedure that he or she is unable to complete. These possibilities should be considered in the treatment planning.

When the clinical health psychologist has had insufficient time to establish adequate rapport with the patient prior to discharge, it is unlikely that the patient will continue with treatment on an outpatient basis. Further, given that most psychological interventions take time, the patient could be discharged believing that interactions with the psychologist had little or no effect, or hope of effect, on her or his health. This, then, colors the patient's perceptions of the relevance of psychology in the future.

An additional source of premature termination or separation is created by training schedules and training rotations. In large teaching institutions, psychological interns or postdoctoral students typically rotate through various psychological subspecialties. To help eliminate some of the problems associated with this issue of "temporary therapists," we have found it helpful to clearly state early in the therapy process the time limits imposed by these conditions and to offer the patient reasonable alternatives (e.g., delay onset of treatment, transfer to another trainee, transfer to staff personnel).

ISSUES OF DISPOSITION

Within an inpatient setting, the goal of the initial interview is to obtain enough information to respond to the consultee's request. This does not mean that the consultation will necessarily be answered in full, but it does mean that the consultee is responded to in a timely fashion. In practicing within an outpatient setting, the consultant is more likely to base case disposition on a number of interviews; thus, the initial communication might reflect a more complete workup of the case.

When physicians consult one another, the consultant typically responds with some objective data and then an opinion. This holds true for lab results, X-ray readings, and physical exams. The same expectations are made of psychologists. However, because we often do not have the same type of diagnostic tools available, we find ourselves limited in the type of information we can provide the referral source. Often our opinion rests on an interview with the patient and a detailed history. At other times, our opinions are based on psychometric evaluation. When testing is involved, we rarely, if ever, provide the physician with testing scores, offering, instead, a summary of interpretations. As a consequence, our opinions and statements need to be presented in a sound manner that reflects an understanding of the patient and the relevant issues.

Communication of Results

In an inpatient setting—whether or not the initial contact results in a case conceptualization—the clinician needs to communicate the disposition of the case to the referral source. Ideally this is done in both verbal and written reports. However, given the frequent unavailability of staff due to conflicting schedules and shift changes, it is often impossible to communicate directly. Consequently, the written report becomes paramount to good communication.

Whether the patient is seen in an inpatient or outpatient setting, a note is either placed in the Progress Notes section of the patient's medical records or written on a separate Consultation Report and placed in the patient's chart. Although settings can differ, some typical house rules require that chart entries be made only in black ink. It is usually prohibited to leave spaces between entries and to black- or white-out errors. When errors occur, a *single-line* mark through them, accompanied by the writer's initials, is required. Only approved abbreviations may be utilized. Progress notes often require not only date of service but also time and length. Although such regulations appear picayune at first, they have developed over time in response to specific needs or problems. They are codified in either JCAH standards or local rules and regulations; infractions are actually monitored by special committees.

If the clinician attempted to meet with the patient and was unable to complete the assessment, a note so indicating should be placed in the medical chart. Although this could initially appear to be a trivial exercise, it is important to communicate to the referral source that an attempt was made to respond to the consultation request. Failure to chart interactions with patients and staff can result in professionally embarrassing situations. Once we encountered a politically difficult situation in which a member of the psychiatry staff, who usually does not see medically ill patients, was seeing a patient at bedside during a difficult hospitalization involving chemotherapy. Because the clinician was unfamiliar with protocol, he had not been documenting these contacts in the medical records. The attending physician was unaware that the patient was receiving these services and requested psychological evaluation and treatment for depressed mood and anxiety. Although duplication in services was avoided, professional embarrassment was not.

Of course the content of the report largely depends on the referral question. As previously emphasized, however, "psychobabble" tends only to infuriate medical personnel, and fosters the belief that psychology has nothing of practical value to offer. The report should be brief, succinct, relevant, and practical, and have explanatory value. It is customary to include an overview of the presenting problem, behavioral observations and mental-status information, relevant biopsychosocial interactions, patient strengths and problem areas, impressions, and recommendations.

Recommendations should include a specific treatment or management plan. Even when no treatment is indicated, the clinician should indicate, when appropriate, the implications of the findings for medical management and for the behavior of health care providers. Psychiatric diagnosis might or might not be included in the written consultation, depending on the nature of the consultation, the rules of the setting, and personal preference. In general, however, diagnostic labels, in and of themselves, are of little value to the consultee and are sometimes viewed with disdain by medical–surgical physicians. Also, they can be latched onto by medical personnel in such a way that the patient becomes defined by his or her diagnosis. There is always concern as to how much and what type of information to reveal in medical charts, written reports, and verbal communications. It is not uncommon for medical personnel to fix their attention on key words in an assessment summary and miss or de-emphasize important subtleties. The following example of a poorly written summary demonstrates this issue:

> The patient was a 49-year-old, Black male with recent onset of cardiac arrythmias. Psychological testing reveals that this patient does not have limited intellectual abilities. This patient behaves in a manner consistent with Type A behavior, and is likely to react in a hostile, competitive manner when his goals are thwarted.

First, it is likely that the reader will miss the "does not" that precedes a description of intelligence. Consequently, this patient might be perceived to have limited intellectual understanding. *Second*, it is quite possible that the reader will not focus on the fact that Type A behaviors are elicited *under certain conditions* and not under all circumstances. As a result, staff could attribute to this man qualities that do not exist.

Knowing When to Refer

Being alert to possible changes or oversights in medical conditions is a responsibility of the clinical health psychologist. When the clinician suspects that the patient is behaving in a manner suggestive of organic disease, or symptoms described by the patient point to such a case, it is imperative that the psychologist pursue medical evaluation. Consider the following example:

> The patient was a 34-year-old single Caucasian woman who self-referred to a clinical health psychologist for treatment of her bruxing problem. She desired "hypnosis" and "biofeedback" specifically, to stop the clenching and associated pain. The patient described symptoms of tension and pain in the jaw muscles and of congestion in the nasal passages and stated that her palate felt like a "piece of hard steel." The psychologist insisted upon an ear, nose, and throat medical evaluation prior to beginning treatment. A nasopharyngeal tumor was discovered upon this exam, and radium-implant therapy was begun immediately.

This example illustrates how important assessment of biological targets can be. Patients often do not want to complete medical and dental evaluations because they desire to get on with treatment. It is imperative that this issue be routinely addressed, and, as indicated previously, the clinician might find himself or herself acting in an advocacy role on occasion to be sure that this is accomplished.

In other circumstances, the patient might have had a thorough medical workup that yielded negative physical results, yet she or he continues to report symptoms suggestive of an undocumented organic disease. This type of situation requires the clinical health psychologist to carefully document the patient's symptoms while pursuing further medical evaluations. The psychologist should not be intimidated by medical personnel or hard data attesting to lack of organic disease. In more than one case, the insistence on repeated medical evaluations has resulted in diagnoses of initial stages of disease.

Follow-Up and Follow-Through

Rarely is the single interview or single assessment process sufficient to answer the referral question. As a result, the clinical health psychologist typically allows for *follow-up* procedures. Usually this contact involves additional assessment procedures, some form of intervention, and evaluation as to the effectiveness of an intervention. Unfortunately, follow-up procedures are not always completed. This happens for a variety of reasons including premature discharge of the patient, failure of the clinician to recognize the need for follow-up, and reluctance by the patient to provide further information.

In some packaged treatment programs, there is no provision for outpatient follow-up after discharge from the program. This occurs if follow-up is not viewed as necessary, if follow-up procedures are seen as not cost-effective, or if follow-up sessions are not defined as treatment and thus hold little interest for both patient and clinician.

Follow-through refers to ensuring that necessary or recommended procedures have been executed. It is not uncommon for the clinical health psychologist to recommend that another service, such as social work or psychiatry, also be consulted on behalf of the patient and his or her family. Although this information is typically related through medical-chart progress notes and consultation forms, it is not adequate to assume that the recommended action will automatically occur. Thus, the clinician needs to make direct contact with allied services and continue to follow progress in that department, sometimes coordinating types of services.

Obviously not all problem areas have been discussed in this chapter. However, the information presented will alert the reader to common pitfalls in practice.

Chapter 9
Future Issues for Clinical Health Psychology

The future of clinical health psychology will depend upon the course of events within the field itself, as well as upon those external to the discipline of psychology. In this chapter we shall elucidate some of the trends and changes we anticipate and provide our perceptions of their potential impact. Our purpose is to stimulate thinking, discussion, and research related to these issues rather than to detail particular positions.

TECHNOLOGICAL ADVANCES

The field of clinical health psychology will become increasingly technology-oriented. More and more assessment tools will be computerized and easily available to nonpsychologist users, sometimes bypassing local psychologists within the health care system. With this change will come the potential for increased abuse of such services, especially given the absence of psychometrically and clinically trained professionals in the interpretation process at the clinical case level. To the extent that diagnostic labels are rendered or treatment decisions are actually made utilizing such data, there will be increased risks of malpractice suits involving these techniques. Given this, and the fact that at present there are few measures that are adequately normed for work with medical–surgical patients, we could witness in health care the kind of backlash about testing that occurred within the school system surrounding the use of intelligence tests. Psychologists might need to take an increased role in professional and patient advocacy with respect to this issue.

Another area of technological advance has to do with increased sophistication in psychophysiological measurement. Developments in ambulatory monitoring will permit more accurate psychophysiological profiling and assessment and, perhaps, even *in vivo* treatment programming. The potential exists for developing a considerable data base for the biopsycho-social model in the real world, data that are currently lacking, and for facilitating generalization of treatment efforts.

As clinical health psychologists contribute their expertise in behavior change to the health care system, there are also more opportunities for coercive control of patients, to make them comply with the values of health care providers. Although Weiss (1982), in his 1980 Presidential Address to the Division of Health Psychology, warned about "technology run amok" (given its inherent amorality), there still remains little focus in the literature on ethical issues in clinical health psychology. We encourage more attention to this area and hope that our chapter 4 will stimulate increased discussion.

DEVELOPMENT OF THE PROFESSION

Specialization

As the field develops, there will be increased need for specialization within clinical health psychology. This is already apparent with respect to pediatric psychology and clinical neuropsychology, and will also become evident within other areas. We have repeatedly indicated that it is impossible for the clinical health psychologist to have in-depth knowledge and clinical expertise in the biopsychosocial aspects of such diverse areas as biofeedback for cardiac arrhythmias, treatment of chronic pain, genetic counseling, organ-donor evaluations, and death and dying. However, we believe that predoctorial training should continue to be generic in both clinical psychology and health psychology and that specialization should occur at the postdoctorial level. This will avoid the production of "blacksmiths" who might be quickly outdated without a firm grounding in the discipline of psychology. Along with this trend, there will be increased attention to issues of accreditation and credential-ing.

With this increased specialization comes the risk that patients will be "chunked" into health behavior patterns. Clinicians might take a myopic view in the same manner that physicians have been accused of doing, given that profession's specialization around organ systems. Thus we could have weight management psychologists, Type A psychologists, stress management psychologists, and so forth. We might attempt to simplistically treat "smoking behavior" without a full appreciation of the context of this behavior within the individual and his or her environment. This results in a split similar to the mind–body dualism for which we have criticized medicine. This new dualism might be called *behavior–person* dualism. If followed, at best our treatments will be ineffective in the long run; at worst, we will cause damage to our patients. We fully agree that the focus in clinical health psychology is not upon psychopathology, but we deplore the comments of health psychologists suggesting that expertise in this area is not important. The clinical health psychologist must understand behavior and behavior change within both "normal" and "abnormal" domains.

Professional Practice

In the area of practice, we anticipate an increase in cross referrals among psychologists and a more prominent focus on training other disciplines in the delivery of specialized services as new information becomes available. We believe that psychology has the potential to survive current health care industry crises primarily because of our expertise in research, program development and evaluation, and measurement of behavior. Other disciplines will assume roles as therapists and do so less expensively. Unfortunately, our recent experiences with hiring suggest that many psychologists entering practice now see themselves primarily as therapists and have little other training. Because policymakers in large organizations cannot appreciate important distinctions *within* psychology, we might fail to live up to our potential in the health care system because of our own complacency, at least until recently, about the reliability of the product of graduate training.

Growth of Knowledge

Despite our adherence to the biopsychosocial model, we agree with Schwartz (1982), who pointed out that, as yet, there is no empirical evidence that use of this model leads to better diagnoses or better treatments for patients. In general, the field is lacking in the well-controlled clinical trials needed to assess costs, benefits, and side effects of various intervention strategies. (As the newcomer in health care, our discipline shall be held to a higher standard than current medical practices!) We anticipate more interdisciplinary clinical research and, thus, more rigorous searches for interactions among biological, psychological, and social interventions.

Related to this, we are concerned about the number of psychologists entering practice who come from training programs that have provided no substantial background in conducting or evaluating clinical research. Not only will these psychologists be unable to contribute to the body of knowledge, but they will also lack the expertise to critically review current findings and make informed decisions about applications. They could therefore unwittingly contribute to a backlash in many areas of clinical health psychology, such as we have already experienced to some extent in biofeedback and wellness programs. Our focus on self-control and the popularization of related techniques has already produced a new clinical problem to deal with: the patient who feels guilty and incompetent that she or he cannot will her or his cancer away, or bring all psychophysiological symptoms under control. We must not promise more than we can deliver, either in terms of quantity of service or power of our techniques.

CHANGES IN PSYCHIATRY

The solution to psychiatry's identity problem has been the "remedicalization" of the field, due perhaps as much to economics and need to realign with medicine as to scientific developments in biological psychiatry. This trend toward a reaffirmation of the biological factors in mental illness and a focus on psychopharmacology increases opportunities for nonmedical providers of psychological services. In addition, to the extent that psychologists continue to be trained in areas relevant to health care systems that their psychiatric colleagues are not (e.g., research, program evaluation, measurement of behavior), they will be assured roles on the health care team. Psychiatry continues, as does traditional clinical psychology, to be viewed as being preoccupied with mental illness. Thus, the role of clinical health psychology is ripe for development. However, the increased competition in the health care industry could result in increased interprofessional conflict.

CHANGES IN THE HEALTH CARE SYSTEM

The health care system in the United States is undergoing a major revolution in response to cost-containment reform. With respect to federal programs, prospective payment systems and fixed-rate reimbursement for DRGs are having significant effects upon hospital practices. The legislation affecting health care evolves through the political process, about which many psychologists tend to be either naive or uninterested. In our opinion, to insure survival, clinical health psychologists need to become politically involved in health policy at both institutional and legislative levels.

In the private sector, it appears that corporate America is going to control the health care delivery system and that business interests will dictate quality of care. Cummings (1986) pointed out that "psychologists are ill prepared for the competitive market for their services that lies ahead" (p. 426). In his treatise on "The Dismantling of Our Health System," he pointed out how psychologists have historically eschewed marketing of their products and been overly committed to notions of *cure* rather than "brief intermittent psychotherapy throughout the life cycle" (p. 429). To survive as a practicing clinical health psychologist, it is becoming clear that sophistication in HMOs and preferred provider organizations (PPOs) will be required, as it is estimated that the majority of Americans will be obtaining their health care through such organizations by the mid 1990s. Although this issue has not been addressed in graduate education to date, psychologists will need to develop skills in dealing with corporate administrative structures, in providing evidence of accountability, and in using management information systems for cost–benefit analyses. The future will undoubtedly be challenging!

SUGGESTED READINGS

Bradley, L. A., Prokop, C. K., & Clayman, D. A. (1981). Medical psychology and behavioral medicine: Summary and future concerns. In C. K. Prokop & L. A. Bradley (Eds.), *Medical psychology: Contributions to behavioral medicine*. New York: Academic.

Cummings, N. A. (1986). The dismantling of our health care system. *American Psychologist, 41*, 426–431.

REFERENCES

Ader, R. (1981). *Psychoneuroimmunology*. New York: Academic.

Agras, W. S. (1984). The behavioral treatment of somatic disorders. In W. D. Gentry (Ed.), *Handbook of behavioral medicine*. New York: Guilford.

Alexander, F. (1950). *Psychosomatic Medicine*. New York: Norton.

American Psychiatric Association. (1980). *Diagnostic and statistical manual of mental disorders (3rd ed)*. Washington, DC: Author.

American Psychological Association. (1981). Ethical principles of psychologists. *American Psychologist 36*, 633–638.

American Psychological Association. (1985a). *A hospital practice primer for psychologists*. Washington, DC: Author.

American Psychological Association. (1985b). *Standards for educational and psychological testing*. Washington, DC: Author.

American Psychological Association. (1985c). *Standards for providers of psychological services (rev. 7th draft)*. Washington, DC: Author.

American Psychological Association. (1986). *Accreditation handbook*. Washington, DC: Author.

Asken, M. J. (1979). Medical psychology: Toward definition, clarification, and organization. *Professional Psychology, 10*, 66–73.

Bagheri, A. S., Lane, L. S., Kline, F. M., & Araujo, D. M. (1981). Why physicians fail to tell patients a psychiatrist is coming. *Psychosomatics, 22*(5), 407–419.

Baker v. United States, 226 F. Supp. 129 (S.D. Iowa 1964).

Bandura, A. (1969). *Principles of behavior modification*. New York: Holt, Rinehart and Winston.

Barton, W. E., & Sanborn, C. J. (1978). *Law and the mental health professional*. New York: International Universities Press.

Bazelon, D. L. (1974). Psychiatrists and the adversary process. *Scientific American, 290*, 18–23.

Beck, A. T. (1972). *Depression: Causes and treatment*. Philadelphia: University of Pennsylvania Press.

Beck, A. T., Rush, A. J., Shaw, B. F., & Emery, G. (1979). *Cognitive therapy of depression*. New York: Guilford.

Beecher, H. K. (1956). Relationship of the significance of wound to the pain experienced. *Journal of the American Medical Association, 161*, 1609–1613.

Beigler, J. S. (1984). Tarasoff v. confidentiality. *Behavioral Sciences and the Law, 2*, 273–289.

Belar, C. D. (1980). Training the clinical psychology student in behavioral medicine. *Professional Psychology, 11*(4), 620–627.

Belar, C. D. (in press). The current status of predoctoral and postdoctoral training in health psychology. In G. C. Stone, S. M. Weiss, J. D. Matarazzo, N. E. Miller, J. Rodin, C. D. Belar, M. J. Follick, & J. E. Singer (Eds.), *Health psychology: A discipline and a profession*. Chicago: University of Chicago Press.

140

Belar, C. D., & Kibrick, S. (1986). Biofeedback in the treatment of chronic back pain. In A. Holzman & D. Turk (Eds.), *Pain management: A handbook of psychological treatment approaches.* New York: Pergamon Press.

Belar, C. D., & Siegel, L. J. (1983). A survey of postdoctoral training programs in health psychology. *Health Psychology, 2*(4), 413–425.

Belar, C. D., & Siegel, L. J. (1984). *Directory of postdoctoral training in health psychology.* Washington, DC: American Psychological Association.

Belar, C. D., & Tavel, E. B. (1982). *Directory of health psychology training opportunities in doctoral psychology programs.* Washington, DC: American Psychological Association.

Belar, C. D., Wilson, E., & Hughes, H. (1982). Health psychology training in doctoral psychology programs. *Health Psychology, 1*(3), 289–299.

Bergner, M., Bobbitt, R. A., Carter, W. B., & Gilson, B. S. (1981). The Sickness Impact Profile: Development and final revision of a health status measure. *Medical Care, 19,* 787–806.

Berman, P. S., & Johnson, H. J. (1985). A psychophysiological assessment battery. *Biofeedback and Self-Regulation, 10*(3), 203–221.

Bernstein, D. A., & Borkovec, T. D. (1973). *Progressive Relaxation Training: A manual for the helping professions.* Champaign, IL: Research Press.

Berry v. Moench, 8 Utah 2d 191, 331 P2d 814 (1958).

Billowitz, A., & Friedson, W. (1978–1979). Are psychiatric consultants' recommendations followed? *International Journal of Psychiatry in Medicine, 9*(2), 179–189.

Binner, P. R. (1986). DRGs and the administration of mental health services. *American Psychologist, 41,* 64–69.

Blanchard, E. B., & Andrasik, F. (1985). *Management of chronic headaches: A psychological approach.* Elmsford, NY: Pergamon.

Bradley, L. A., Prokop, C. K., Gentry, W. D., Van Der Heide, L. H., & Prieto, E. J. (1980). Assessment of chronic pain. In C. K. Prokop & L. A. Bradley (Eds.), *Medical psychology: Contributions to behavioral medicine.* New York: Academic.

Brodman, K., Erdman, A. J., & Wolff, H. G. (1949). *Cornell Medical Index Health Questionnaire.* New York: Cornell University Medical College.

Bursztajn, H., Gutheil, T. G., Hamm, R. M., & Brodsky, A. (1983). Subjective data and suicide assessment in the light of recent legal developments: Part II. Clinical uses of legal standards in the interpretation of subjective data. *International Journal of Law and Psychiatry, 6,* 331–350.

Cacioppo, J. T., Petty, R. E., & Marshall-Goodell, B. (1985). Physical, social, and inferential elements of psychophysiological measurement. In P. Karoly (Ed.), *Measurement strategies in health psychology.* New York: John Wiley & Sons.

Carrington, C. (Ed.) (1986). *Internship programs in professional psychology 1986–87,* 15th Ed. Washington, DC: Association of Psychology Internship Centers.

Cassileth, B. R., Zupkis, R. V., Sutton-Smith, K., & March, V. (1980). Informed consent: Why are its goals imperfectly realized? *The New England Journal of Medicine, 302,* 896–900.

Cattell, R. B., Eber, H. W., & Tatsouka, M. M. (1970). *Handbook for the Sixteen Personality Factor Questionnaire (16PF).* Champaign, IL: Institute for Personality and Ability Testing.

Cautela, J. R. (1967). Covert sensitization. *Psychological Reports, 20,* 459–468.

Cohen, R. J. (1979). *Malpractice: A guide for mental health professionals.* New York: The Free Press.

Cohen, R. J. & Mariano, W. E. (1982). *Legal guidebook in mental health.* New York: The Free Press.

Corah, N. L. (1969). Development of a dental anxiety scale. *Journal of Dental Research, 48,* 396.

Cross, H. K., & Deardorff, W. W. (1987). Malpractice in psychotherapy and psychological evaluation. In J. R. McNamara & M. Appel (Eds.), *Critical issues, developments, and trends in professional psychology, Vol. 3.* New York: Praeger.

Cummings, N. A. (1986). The dismantling of our health care system. *American Psychologist,* 41(4) 426–431.

Davis, M., Eshelman, E. R., & McKay, M. (1980). *The relaxation and stress reduction workbook.* Richmond, CA: New Harbinger.

Dawidoff, D. (1966). The malpractice of psychiatrists. *Duke Law Journal,* 696–716.

Deardorff, W. W., Cross, H. J., & Hupprich, W. (1984). Malpractice liability in psychotherapy: Client and practitioner perspectives. *Professional Psychology: Research and Practice,* 15, 590–600.

DeGood, D. E. (1983). Reducing medical patients' reluctance to participate in psychotherapies: The initial session. *Professional Psychology: Research & Practice,* 14(5), 570–579.

DePiano, F. A., & Selzberg, H. C. (1979). Clinical applications of hypnosis to three psychosomatic disorders. *Psychological Bulletin,* 86, 1223–1235.

Derogatis, L. R. (1977). *SCL-90-R (Revised Version Manual-1).* Baltimore: Author.

Derogatis, L. R. (1986). The psychosocial adjustment to illness scale (PAIS). *Journal of Psychosomatic Research,* 30(1), 77–91.

Dorland's Illustrated Medical Dictionary (26th ed). (1981). Philadelphia: W. B. Saunders.

Dubin, S. S. (1972). Obsolescence or lifelong education: A choice for the professional. *American Psychologist,* 27, 486–496.

Elfant, A. B. (1985). Psychotherapy and assessment in hospital settings: Ideological and professional conflicts. *Professional Psychology: Research and Practice,* 16(1), 55–63.

Ellis, A. (1962). *Reason and emotion in psychotherapy.* New York: Lyle Stuart.

Engel, G. L. (1977). The need for a new medical model: A challenge for biomedicine. *Science,* 196(4286), 129–136.

Fabrega, H. (1974). *Disease and social behavior.* Cambridge, MA: MIT Press.

Feldman, S. R., & Ward, T. M. (1979). Psychotherapeutic injury: Reshaping the implied contract as an alternative to malpractice. *North Carolina Law Review,* 58, 63–96.

Feuerstein, M., Labbé, E. E., & Kuczmierczyk, A. R. (1986). *Health psychology: A psychobiological perspective.* New York: Plenum.

Fisher, K. (1985). Malpractice: Charges catch clinicians in cycle of shame, slip-ups. *American Psychological Association Monitor,* 16, 6–7.

Folstein, M. F., Folstein, S. E., & McHugh, P. R. (1975). "Mini-mental-state": A practical method for grading the cognitive state of patients for the clinician. *Journal of Psychological Research,* 12, 189–198.

Fordyce, W. E. (1976). *Behavioral methods for chronic pain and illness.* St. Louis: C. V. Mosby.

Fowler, R. D., & Butcher, J. N. (1986). Critique of Matarazzo's views on computerized testing: All sigma and no meaning. *American Psychologist,* 41, 64–96.

Frank, J. D. (1973). *Persuasion and healing (Rev. ed.).* Baltimore: Johns Hopkins University Press.

Furniss v. Fitchett, N.Z.L.R. 396 S. Ct. (1958).

Furrow, B. (1980). *Malpractice in psychotherapy.* Lexington, MA: D. C. Heath.

Gable, R. K. (1983). Malpractice liability of psychologists. In B. D. Sales, (Ed.) *The professional psychologist's handbook.* New York: Plenum.

Gentry, W. D. (Ed.) (1984). *Handbook of behavioral medicine.* New York: Guilford.

Gentry, W. D., & Matarazzo, J. D. (1981). Medical psychology: Three decades of growth and development. In C. K. Prokop, & L. A. Bradley (Eds.), *Medical psychology: Contributions to behavioral medicine.* New York: Academic.

Gentry, W. D., Street, W. J., Masur, F. T., & Asken, M. J. (1981). Training in medical psychology: A survey of graduate and internship training programs. *Professional Psychology,* 13, 397–403.

Gil, K. (1984). Coping effectively with invasive medical procedures: A descriptive model. *Clinical Psychology Review,* 4, 339–362.

Goldfried, M. R., & Davison, G. (1976). *Clinical behavior therapy.* New York: Holt, Rinehart and Winston.

Goodstein, L. D. (1985). *White paper on duty to protect.* Washington, DC: American Psychological Association Committee on Legal Issues.

Graham, J. R. (1977). *The MMPI: A practical guide.* New York: Oxford University Press.

Greenberg, S. (1986). The supportive approach to therapy. *Clinical Social Work Journal, 14*(1), 6–13.

Greene, R. L. (1980). *The MMPI: An interpretive manual.* New York: Grune & Stratton.

Grimaldi, K. E., & Lichtenstein, E. (1969). Hot, smoky air as an aversive stimulus in the treatment of smoking. *Behaviour Research and Therapy, 7,* 275–282.

Gruen, W. (1975). Effects of brief psychotherapy during the hospitalization period on the recovery process in heart attacks. *Journal of Consulting and Clinical Psychology, 43,* 223–232.

Grunder, T. M. (1980). On the readability of surgical consent forms. *The New England Journal of Medicine, 302,* 900–902.

Guggenheim, F. G. (1978). Suicide. In T. P. Hackett & N. H. Cassen (Eds.), *Massachusetts General Hospital: Handbook of general hospital psychiatry.* St. Louis: C.V. Mosby.

Gutheil, T. G., Bursztajn, H., Hamm, R. M., & Brodsky, A. (1983). Subjective data and suicide assessment in the light of recent legal developments: Part I. Malpractice prevention and the use of subjective data. *International Journal of Law and Psychiatry, 6,* 317–329.

Halperin, D. A. (1980). "Misinformed consent." *Bulletin of the American Academy of Psychiatry and Law, 8,* 175–178.

Hamilton, M. (1959). The assessment of anxiety status by rating. *British Journal of Medical Psychology, 32,* 50–55.

Hammer v. Rosen, 7 N.Y.2d 376. 165 N.E.2d 756. 198 N.Y.S.2d (1960).

Harris, M. (1973). Tort liability of the psychotherapist. *University of San Francisco Law Review, 8,* 405–436.

Hathaway, S. R., & McKinley, J. C. (1967). *The Minnesota Multiphasic Personality Inventory Manual.* New York: Psychological Corp.

Heide, F. J., & Borkovec, T. D. (1984). Relaxation-induced anxiety: Mechanisms and theoretical implications. *Behavior Research and Therapy, 22*(1), 1–12.

Hofer, P. J., & Bersoff, D. N. (1983). *Standards for the administration and interpretation of computerized psychological testing.* Available from D. N. Bersoff, Suite 511, 1200 Seventeenth Street N.W, Washington, DC 20036.

Hogan, D. (1979). *The regulation of psychotherapists: Vol. 3. A review of malpractice suits in the United States.* Cambridge, MA: Ballinger.

Holmes, T. H., & Rahe, R. H. (1967). A social readjustment rating scale. *Journal of Psychosomatic Research, 11,* 213–218.

Holzman, A. D., & Turk, D. C. (1986). Pain management: A handbook of *psychological treatment approaches.* Elmsford, NY: Pergamon.

Jablonski by Pahls v. United States, 712 F.2d 391 (1983).

Jacobs, D. F. (1983). The development and application of Standards of Practice for Professional Psychologists. In B. D. Sales (Ed.), *The professional psychologists' handbook.* New York: Plenum.

Jacobs, J., Bernhard, R., Delgado, A., & Strain, J. J. (1977). Screening for organic mental syndromes in the medically ill. *Annals of Internal Medicine, 86,* 40.

Jacobson, E. (1939). *Progressive relaxation.* Chicago: University of Chicago Press.

Janis, I. L. (1958). *Psychological stress: Psychoanalytic and behavioral studies of surgical patients.* New York: Wiley.

Jenkins, C. D., Zyzanski, S. J. & Rosenman, R. H. (1979). *Jenkins Activity Survey Manual.* New York: The Psychological Corporation.

Joint Commission on Accreditation of Hospitals. (1983). *Consolidated standards manual for child, adolescent, and adult psychiatric, alcoholism, and drug abuse facilities.* Chicago, IL: Author.

Joint Commission on Accreditation of Hospitals. (1984) *Accreditation manual for hospitals.* Chicago, IL: Author.

Jones, E. & Nisbett, R. (1971). The actor and observer: Divergent perceptions of the causes of behavior. In E. E. Jones, D. E. Kanouse, H. H. Kelly, R. E. Nisbett, S. Valins, & B. Weiner (Eds.), *Attribution: Perceiving the causes of behavior.* Morristown, NJ: General Learning Press.

Kamenar, P. D. (1984). Psychiatrists' duty to warn of a dangerous patient: A survey of the law. *Behavioral Sciences and the Law, 2,* 259–272.

Karoly, P. (Ed.) (1985). *Measurement strategies in health psychology.* New York: John Wiley & Sons.

Katz, S. T., Downs, H., Cash, H., & Grotz, R. (1970). Progress in the development of the index of ADL. *The Gerontologist, 10,* 20–30.

Keefe, F. J., & Blumenthal, J. A. (Eds.) (1982). *Assessment strategies in behavioral medicine.* New York: Grune & Stratton.

Keith-Spiegel, P., & Koocher, G. P. (1985). *Ethics in psychology.* New York: Random House.

Kendall, P. C., & Watson, D. (1981). Psychological preparation for stressful medical procedures. In C. K. Prokop & L. A. Bradley (Eds.), *Medical psychology: Contributions to behavioral medicine.* New York: Academic.

Klein, J. I., & Glover, S. I. (1983). Psychiatric malpractice. *International Journal of Law and Psychiatry, 6,* 131–157.

Kleinman, A., Eisenberg, L., & Good, B. (1977). *Culture, illness, and care: Clinical lessons from anthropological and cross-cultural research.* Unpublished report.

Knapp, S. (1980). A primer on malpractice for psychologists. *Professional Psychology, 11,* 606–612.

Knapp, S., & Vandecreek, L. (1981). Behavioral medicine: Its malpractice risks for psychologists. *Professional Psychology, 12,* 677–683.

Koocher, G. P. (1983). Ethical and professional standards in psychology. In B. D. Sales (Ed.), *The professional psychologist's handbook.* New York: Plenum.

Korchin, S. J. (1976). *Modern clinical psychology.* New York: Basic Books.

Lang, P. J., & Melamed, B. G. (1969). Avoidance conditioning therapy of an infant with chronic ruminative vomiting. *Journal of Abnormal Psychology, 74,* 139–142.

LeCron, L. (1970). *Self hypnosis.* New York: New American Library.

Leigh, H., & Reiser, M. F. (1980). *Biological, psychological, and social dimensions of medical practice.* New York: Plenum.

Leo, J. (1984, October). Polling for mental health. *Time,* pp. 80.

Ley, P. (1982). Studies of recall in medical settings. *Human Learning, 1,* 223–233.

Lipowski, Z. J. (1967). Review of consultation psychiatry and psychosomatic medicine: I. General principles. *Psychosomatic Medicine, 29*(2), 153–171.

Lipowski, Z. J. (1977). Psychosomatic medicine in the seventies: An overview. *American Journal of Psychiatry, 134*(3) 233–243.

Loeser, J. KD. (1986). Herpes Zoster and postherpetic neuralgia. *Pain, 25,* 149–164.

Lucente, F. E., & Fleck, S. (1972). A study of hospitalization anxiety in 408 medical and surgical patients. *Psychosomatic Medicine, 34*(4), 304–312.

Magrab, P. R., & Papadopoulou, Z. L. (1977). The effect of a token economy on dietary compliance for children on hemodialysis. *Journal of Applied Behavior Analysis, 10,* 573–578.

Malament, I. B., Dunn, M. E., & Davis, R. (1975). Pressure sores: An operant conditioning approach to prevention. *Archives of Physical Medicine and Rehabilitation, 56,* 161–165.

Markus, R. M. (1965). Conspiracy of silence. *Cleveland Law Review, 14,* 520–533.

Matarazzo, J. D. (1980). Behavioral health and behavioral medicine. *American Psychologist, 35,* 807–817.

Matarazzo, J. D. (1983b). Education and training in health psychology: Boulder or Bolder. *Health Psychology*, 2(1), 73–113.

Matarazzo, J. D. (1983a). Computerized psychological testing. *Science, 221*, 323.

Matarazzo, J. D. (1986). Computerized clinical psychological test interpretation: Unvalidated plus all mean and no sigma. *American Psychologist, 41*, 14–21.

Matthews, K. (1982). Psychological perspectives on the Type A behavior pattern. *Psychological Bulletin, 91*, 293–323.

McKay, M., Davis, M., & Fanning, P. (1981). *Thoughts and Feelings: The art of cognitive stress intervention*. Richmond, CA: New Harbinger.

Mechanic, D. (1972). Social psychological factors affecting the presentation of bodily complaints. *New England Journal of Medicine, 286*, 1132–1139.

Meenan, R. F., Gertman, P. M., & Mason, J. H. (1982). The arthritis impact measurement scales: Further investigation of a health status measure. *Arthritis and Rheumatology, 25*, 1048–1053.

Meichenbaum, D. (1977). *Cognitive behavior modification: An integrative approach*. New York: Plenum.

Melamed, B. G., & Siegel, L. J. (1980). *Behavioral Medicine: Practical applications in health care*. New York: Springer.

Melzack, R. (1975). The McGill Pain questionnaire: Major properties and scoring methods. *Pain, 1*, 277–299.

Melzack, R., & Wall, P. D. (1983). *The challenge of pain*. New York: Basic Books.

Merck Manual (14th ed). (1984). Rahway, NJ: Merck Co.

Miller, T. W. (1981). Professional services evaluation in a medical setting. In C. K. Prokop & L. A. Bradley (Eds.), *Medical psychology: Contributions to behavioral medicine*. New York: Academic.

Millon, T. (1982). On the nature of clinical health psychology. In T. Millon, C. J. Green, & R. B. Meagher (Eds.), *Handbook of clinical health psychology*. New York: Plenum.

Millon, T., Green, C. J., & Meagher, R. B., (Eds.) (1982). *Handbook of clinical health psychology*. New York: Plenum.

Millon, T., Green, C. J., & Meagher, R. B. (1982b). *Millon Behavioral Health Inventory manual*. Minneapolis: National Computer Systems.

Moos, R. H. (1974). *Evaluating treatment environments: A social ecological approach*. New York: Wiley.

Moos, R. H. & (Ed.) (1977). *Coping with physical illness*. New York: Plenum.

Moos, R. H. (1981). *Work Environment Scale manual*. Palo Alto, CA: Consulting Psychologists Press.

Moos, R., & Moos, B. (1981). *Family Environment Scale manual*. Palo Alto, CA: Consulting Psychologists Press.

Morrow, G., & Clayman, D. (1982). *A membership survey of the Division of Health Psychology, American Psychological Association*. Unpublished manuscript.

Murray, H. A. (1938). *Explorations in personality*. New York: Oxford University Press.

Nader, R., Petkas, P., & Blackwell, K. (Eds.) (1972). *Whistle blowing*. New York: Bantam.

Newman, A. S. (1981). Ethical issues in the supervision of psychotherapy. *Professional Psychology, 12*(6), 690–695.

Noll, J. D. (1976). The psychotherapist and informed consent. *American Journal of Psychiatry, 133*, 1451–1453.

Olton, D. S., & Noonberg, A. R. (1980). *Biofeedback: Clinical applications in behavioral medicine*. Englewood Cliffs, NJ: Prentice-Hall.

Osler, W. (1971). In W. P. D. Wrightsman (Ed.), *The emergence of scientific medicine*. Edinburgh: Oliver & Boyd.

Petrucci, R. J., & Harwick, R. D. (1984). Role of the psychologist on a radical head and neck surgical service team. *Professional Psychology, 15*(4), 538–543.

Philips, C. (1978). Tension headache: Theoretical problems. *Behavior Research and Therapy,* *16,* 249–261.

Physician's Desk Reference (40th ed). (1986). Gradell, NJ: Medical Economics.

Pope, K. S., Simpson, H. J., & Myron, M. F. (1978). Malpractice in outpatient psycho-therapy. *American Journal of Psychotherapy, 32,* 593–600.

Professional Negligence. (1973). *University of Pennysylvania Law Review, 121,* 627.

Prokop, C. K., & Bradley, L. A. (Eds.) (1981). *Medical psychology: Contributions to behavioral medicine.* New York: Academic.

Quinn, K. M. (1984). The impact of Tarasoff on clinical practice. *Behavioral Sciences and the Law, 2,* 319–329.

Ray, W. J., Raczynski, J. M., Rogers, T., & Kimball, W. H. (1979). *Evaluation of clinical biofeedback.* New York: Plenum.

Redd, W. H. & Andrykowski, M. A. (1982). Behavioral interventions in cancer treatment: Controlling aversive reactions to chemotherapy. *Journal of Counseling and Clinical Psycho-logy, 50*(6), 1018–1030.

Rorschach, H. (1942). *Psychodiagnostics.* New York: Grune & Stratton.

Rosenbaum, L. (1983). Biofeedback-assisted stress management for insulin-treated diabetes mellitus. *Biofeedback and Self Regulation, 8*(1), 519–532.

Rosenman, R. (1978). the interview method of assessment of the coronary-prone behavior pattern. In T. M. Dembroski, S. M. Weiss, J. L. Shields, S. G. Haynes, & M. Feinleib (Eds.), *Coronary-prone behavior.* New York: Springer-Verlag.

Roy v. Hartogs, 85 Misc.2d 891, 381 N.Y.S.2d 587 (1975).

Russo, D. C., Bird, P. O., & Masek, B. J. (1980). Assessment issues in behavioral medicine. *Behavioral Assessment, 2*(1), 1–18.

Sadoff, R. L. (1979). Changes in mental health law: Progress for patients — problems for psychiatrists. In S. Halleck (Ed.), *New directions for mental health services: Coping with the legal onslaught, No. 4.* San Francisco: Jossey-Bass.

Sajwaj, T., Libet, J., & Agras, W. S. (1974). Lemon juice therapy: The control of life threatening rumination in a six month old infant. *Journal of Applied Behavior Analysis, 7,* 557–566.

Samuels, M., & Samuels, N. (1975). *Seeing with the mind's eye.* New York: Random House.

Sarason, I. G., Johnson, J. H., & Siegel, J. M. (1978). Assessing the impact of life changes: Development of the Life Experiences Survey. *Journey of Consulting and Clinical Psychology, 46,* 932–946.

Schenkenberg, T., Peterson, L., Wood, D., & DaBell, R. (1981). Psychological consultation/ liaison in a medical and neurological setting: Physicians' appraisal. *Professional Psychology, 12*(3), 309–317.

Schindler, R. J. (1976). Malpractice — Another new dimension of liability — a critical analysis. *Trial Lawyer's Guide,* 129–151.

Schofield, W. (1969). The role of psychology in the delivery of health services. *American Psychologist, 24,* 565–584.

Schultz, J. H., & Luthe, W. (1969). *Autogenic therapy.* New York: Grune & Stratton.

Schutz, B. M. (1982). *Legal liability in psychotherapy: A practitioner's guide to risk management.* San Francisco: Jossey-Bass.

Schwartz, G. E. (1982). Testing the biopsychosocial model: The ultimate challenge facing behavioral medicine? *Journal of Consulting and Clinical Psychology, 50,* 1040–1053.

Schwartz, G. E., & Weiss, S. M. (1978). Behavioral medicine revisited: An amended definition. *Journal of Behavioral Medicine, 1,* 249–251.

Schwitzgebel, R. L., & Schwitzgebel, R. K. (1980). *Law and psychological practice.* New York: Wiley.

Seeburg, K. N., & DeBoer, K. F. (1980). Effects of EMG biofeedback on diabetes. *Biofeedback and Self Regulation, 5,* 289–293.

Shapiro, A. K. (1971). *Placebo effects in medicine, psychotherapy and behavior change: An empirical analysis.* New York: John Wiley.

Shevitz, S. A., Silberfarb, P. M., & Lipowski, Z. J. (1976). Psychiatric consultations in a general hospital: A report on 1,000 referrals. *Diseases of the Nervous System, 37*(5), 295–300.

Shows, W. D. (1976). Problem of training psychology interns in medical schools: A case of trying to change the leopard's spots. *Professional Psychology, 7,* 393–395.

Slovenko, R. (1979). Psychotherapy and informed consent: A search in judicial regulation. In W. E. Barton & C. J. Sanborn (Eds.), *Law and the mental health professions.* New York: International Universities Press.

Southard, M. J., & Gross, B. H. (1983). Making clinical decisions after Tarasoff. In B. Gross & I. Weinberger (Eds.), *New directions for mental health services: The mental health professional and the legal system, No. 16.* San Francisco: Jossey-Bass.

Spielberger, C. D., Gorsuch, R. L., & Lushene, R. (1970). *The State-Trait Anxiety Inventory manual.* Palo Alto, CA: Consulting Psychologists Press.

Stabler, B., & Mesibov, G. B. (1984). Role functions of pediatric and health psychologists in health-care settings. *Professional Psychology: Research and Practice, 15*(2), 142–151.

Stone, A. A. (1979). Informed consent: Special problems for psychiatry. *Hospital and Community Psychiatry, 30,* 321–327.

Stone, G. C. (1979). Psychology and the health system. In G. C. Stone, F. Cohen, & N. Adler (Eds.), *Health Psychology: A handbook.* San Francisco: Jossey-Bass.

Stone, G. C. (Ed.). (1983). National working conference on education and training in health psychology. *Health Psychology, 2,* (Suppl.5), 1–153.

Stone, G. C., Cohen, F., & Adler, N. (Eds.) (1979). *Health Psychology: A handbook.* San Francisco: Jossey-Bass.

Stone, G. C., Weiss, S. M., Matarazzo, J. D., Miller, N. E., Rodin, J., Belar, C. D., Follick, M. J., & Singer, J. E. (Eds.) (in press). *Health psychology: A discipline and a profession.* Chicago: University of Chicago Press.

Stricker, G. (1983). Peer review systems in psychology. In B. D. Sales (Ed.), *The professional psychologists' handbook.* New York: Plenum.

Stricker, G., & Cohen, L. H. (1984). APA/CHAMPUS peer review project: Implications for research and practice. *Professional Psychology: Research and Practice, 15,* 96–108.

Sutton, E., & Belar, C. D. (1982). Tension headache patients versus controls: A study of EMG parameters. *Headache,* 133–136.

Swencionis, C., Hall, J. E., & Macklen, R. (in press). Ethical concerns in health psychology. In G. Stone, S. Weiss, J. Matarazzo, N. Miller, J. Rodin, G. Schwartz, C. Belar, M. Follick, & J. Singer (Eds.), *Health psychology: A discipline and a profession.* Chicago: University of Chicago Press.

Tarasoff v. Regents of University of California, 131 Cal. Rptr. 14, 551 P2d 334 (1976).

Tarshis, C. B. (1972). Liability for psychotherapy . *University of Toronto Faculty Law Review, 30,* 75–96.

Theaman, M. (1984). The impact of peer review on professional practice. *American Psychologist, 39,* 406–414.

Tiep, B. L., Burns, M. Kao, D., Madison, R., & Herrera, J. (1986). Biofeedback augmented pursed lips breathing training in patients with chronic obstructive lung disease. Paper presented at the 17th annual meeting of the Biofeedback Society of America. San Francisco, CA.

Turk, D. C., Meichenbaum, D., & Genest, M. (1983). *Pain and behavioral Medicine: A cognitive-behavioral perspective.* New York: Guilford.

Turkington, C. (1986). Response to crisis: Pay up or go naked. *American Psychological Association Monitor, 17,* 6–7.

Warner, R. M. (1982). The psychologist as a social systems consultant. In T. Millon, C. Green, & R. Meagher (Eds.), *Handbook of clinical health psychology.* New York: Plenum.

Weiner, H. (1977). *Psychobiology and human disease*. New York: American Elsevier.

Weisman, A. D. (1978). Coping with illness. In T. P. Hackett & N. H. Cassem (Eds.), *Massachusetts General Hospital Handbook of general hospital psychiatry*. St. Louis: C. V. Mosby.

Weisenberg, M. (1978). Pain and pain control. *Psychological Bulletin, 34*, 1008–1043.

Weiss, S. M. (1982). Health psychology: The time is now. *Health Psychology, 1*(1), 91–91.

Wettstein, R. M. (1984). The prediction of violent behavior and the duty to protect third parties. *Behavioral Sciences and the Law, 2*, 291–317.

Widiger, T. A., & Rorer, L. G. (1984). The responsible psychotherapist. *American psychologist 39*, 503–515.

Williams, R. B., & Gentry, W. D. (1977). *Behavioral approaches to medical treatment*. Cambridge, MA: Ballinger.

Wolff, H. G. (1953). *Stress and disease*. Springfield, IL: Charles C Thomas.

Wolff, H. G., & Wolf, S. (1951). The management of hypertensive patients. In E. T. Bell (Ed.), *Hypertension*. Minneapolis: University of Minnesota Press.

Wolpe, J. (1958). *Psychotherapy by reciprocal inhibition*. Stanford, CA: Stanford University Press.

Wright, R. H. (1981). Psychologists and professional liability (malpractice) insurance. *American Psychologist, 36*, 1484–1493.

Wyngaarden, J. B., & Smith, L. H., Jr. (1985). *Cecil Textbook of Internal Medicine (17th ed)*. Philadelphia: W. B. Saunders.

Zerubavel, E. (1980). The bureaucratization of responsibility: The case of informed consent. *Bulletin of the American Academy of Psychiatry and Law, 8*, 161–167.

APPENDIX A: JOURNALS RELEVANT TO CLINICAL HEALTH PSYCHOLOGY

Given the wide range of special interests among health psychologists, specialty journals (e.g., *Pain*, *Headache*) are not listed. Rather, the following journals reflect general interests in the field.

American Journal of Public Health. Public Health Association, 1015 15th Street NW, Washington, DC 20005. Focus on risk factors, behavioral health, and risk-factor reduction.

Behavioral Medicine Abstracts. Society of Behavioral Medicine, P.O. Box 8530, University Station, Knoxville, TN 37996. Abstracts compiled from recent medical, psychological, and psychiatric journals.

Behavioral Medicine Update. Society of Behavioral Medicine, P.O. Box 8530, University Station, Knoxville, TN 37996. Newsletter with commentaries and area reviews.

Biofeedback and Self-Regulation. Plenum Publishing Corporation, 233 Spring Street, New York, NY 10013. Focus on methods and theory of self-regulation.

Biological Psychology. North-Holland Publishing Company, P.O. Box 211, 1000 AE Amsterdam, The Netherlands. Psychophysiology, biological correlates of psychological states.

British Journal of Medical Psychology. British Psychological Society, St. Andrews House, 48 Princess Road, East, Leicester LE1 7DR, United Kingdom. Psychology as applicable to medicine, psychotherapy.

Health Psychology. Lawrence Erlbaum Associates, 365 Broadway, Hillsdale, NJ 07642. The official journal of the Division of Health Psychology of the American Psychological Association.

International Journal of Psychiatry in Medicine. Baywood Publishing Company, 120 Marine Street, P.O. Box D, Farmingdale, NY 11735. Psychological issues and health and illness.

Journal of Behavioral Medicine. Plenum Publishing Corporation, 233 Spring Street, New York, NY 10013. Interdisciplinary journal.

Journal of Health and Social Behavior. American Sociological Association, 1722 N Street, NW, Washington, DC 20036. Focus on the health care system, organizations and occupations; sociological perspective of health and disease.

Journal of Human Stress. Opinion Publications, Inc., RR1, Box 396, Shelburne Falls, MA 01370. Focuses on the relationship between stress and disease.

Journal of Pediatric Psychology. Plenum Publishing Corporation, 233 Spring Street, New York, NY 10013. Focus on health and illness in children.

Journal of Psychosomatic Research. Pergamon Press, Inc., Maxwell House, Fairview Park, Elmsford, NY 10523. Wide variety of health psychology research.

New England Journal of Medicine. Massachusetts Medical Society, 10 Shattuck Street, Boston, MA 02115. Some articles relevant to risk factors and the relationships between behavior and disease. Review articles and commentaries reflect prevailing attitudes in medicine.

Psychological Bulletin. American Psychological Association, 1200 Seventeenth Street, NW, Washington, DC 20036. Occasional critical review articles relevant to health psychology.

Psychosomatics. Academy of Psychosomatic Medicine, Cliggot Publishing Co., P.O. Box 4010, 500 W. Putnam Avenue, Greenwich, CT 06830. General focus, with numerous case reports.

Psychosomatic Medicine. American Psychosomatic Society, 265 Nassau Road, Roosevelt, NY 11575. Wide variety of health psychology research.

Preventive Medicine. Academic Press, Inc., 111 Fifth Ave., New York, NY 10003. Focus on health promotion and disease prevention.

Psychophysiology. Society for Psychophysiological Research, 2380 Lisa Lane, Madison, WI 53711. Basic and applied research in psychophysiology.

Psychoneuroendocrinology. Pergamon Press, Inc., Maxwell House, Fairview Park, Elmsford, NY 10523. Focus on relationships between behavior and endocrinology.

Social Science and Medicine. Pergamon Press, Inc., Pergamon Press Ltd., Headington Hill Hall, Oxford, England. International health psychology journal.

APPENDIX B: MEDICAL ABBREVIATIONS

This is a list of commonly used medical abbreviations. Although abbreviations tend to be standard across settings, when comparing approved lists from different hospitals, we have sometimes noted different usages. It is imperative that the practitioner obtain the accepted abbreviations prior to writing in any hospital's medical records. It is also important to known the conditions under which these abbreviations are utilized (e.g., usually never in a discharge summaries).

A — assessment
ā — before
AB — abortion
AD — right ear
ADL — activities of daily living
ad lib — at pleasure
AF — atrial fibrillation
AK — above knee
AL — left ear
AMA — against medical advice
ANA — antinuclear factor
ANS — autonomic nervous system
A&P — auscultation and
   percussion
ASA — aspirin
ASCVD — arteriosclerotic heart
   disease
AU — both ears
A&W — alive and well
BAE, BE — barium enema
B/C — birth control

BCP — birth control pills
bid — twice a day
BF — black female
BK — below knee
BM — bowel movement
BMR — basal metabolic rate
BO — bowel obstruction
BOM — bilateral otitis media
BP — blood pressure
BPH — benign prostatic
   hypertrophy
BRP — bathroom privileges
BS — breath sounds
bs — bowel sounds
BSO — bilateral
   salpingo-oophorectomy
BUN — blood urea nitrogen
Bx — biopsy
c̄ — with
CA — carcinoma
Ca — calcium

CAT — computerized axial tomogram
CBC — complete blood count
CC — chief complaint
CCU — coronary care unit
CHD — coronary heart disease
CHF — congestive heart failure
CNS — central nervous system
C/O — complains of
COPD — chronic obstructive pulmonary disease
CP — cerebral palsy
CPR — cardiopulmonary resuscitation
Cr N — cranial nerve
CS, C/S — Cesarean section
CSF — cerebrospinal fluid
CVA — cerebrovascular accident
CVD — cardiovascular disease
Cx — cervix
CXR — chest X ray
d — diastolic
D — dorsal spine
D&C — dilation and curettage
D/C'D — discontinued
DIFF — differential blood count
DM — diabetes mellitus
DOA — dead on arrival
DOB — date of birth
DOE — dyspnea on exertion
DTRs — deep tendon reflexes
Dx — diagnosis
EA — emergency area
ECG — electrocardiogram
EEG — electroencephalogram
EENT — eyes, ears, nose, throat
EMG — electromyogram
ENT — ears, nose, throat
EOM — extraocular movements
ESR — erythrocyte sedimentation rate
EUA — examination under anesthesia

FB — foreign body
FBS — fasting blood sugar
FH — family history
F/U — follow-up
FUO — fever of unknown origin
FVC — forced vital capacity
Fx — fracture
G, Gr — gravida
GB — gallbladder
GC — gonococcus
GE — gastroenterology
GG — gamma globulin
GI — gastrointestinal
gr — grain
GSW — gunshot wound
gt — drop
gtt — drops
GU — genitourinary
HA — headache
HBP — high blood pressure
HEENT — head, ears, eyes, nose, throat
H&L — heart and lungs
HNP — herniated nucleus pulposus
H&P — history and physical
HPI — history of present illness
htn — hypertension
hs — at bedtime
Hx — history
ICU — intensive care unit
ID — intradermal
I&D — incision and drainage
IH — infectious hepatitis
IM — intramuscular
IMP — impression
imp — improved
In situ — in normal position
IOP — intraocular pressure
IPPD — intermittent positive pressure breathing
IUP — intrauterine pregnancy
IV — intravenous

IVP — intravenous pyelogram
JRA — juvenile rheumatoid
  arthritis
KJ — knee jerk
KUB — kidney, ureter, bladder
L&A — light and accommodation
LAB — laboratory results
LAP — laparotomy
LLE — left lower extremity
LLL — left lower lobe
LLQ — left lower quadrant
LMD — local medical doctor
LMP — last menstrual period
LOC — level of consciousness
LP — lumbar puncture
LS — lumbosacral
LSK — liver, spleen, kidney
MH — marital history
MI — myocardial infarction
MM — malignant melanoma
MMR — measles, mumps, and
  rubella immunization
MOD — medical officer of the day
NA — not applicable
NAA — no apparent abnormalities
NB — newborn
NC — No change
N/C — no complaints
NK — not known
NL — normal
NPO — nothing by mouth
NR — nonreactive
NSD — no significant difference
NSR — normal sinus rhythm
NSSP — normal size, shape,
  position
N&V — nausea and vomiting
O — objective
OB — obstetrics
OBS — organic brain syndrome
Od — overdose
od — right eye
OM — otitis media

OPC — outpatient clinic
OS — mouth
os — left eye
ou — both eyes
$\bar{p}$ — after
p — pulse
p — plan
PARA — number of pregnancies
PE — physical examination
PERLA — pupils equal, react to
  light and accommodation
PERRLA — pupils equal, round,
  regular, react to light and
  accommodation
PH — past history
PI — present illness
PID — pelvic inflammatory disease
PM — postmortem
PMH — past medical history
PMT — premenstrual tension
PNS — peripheral nervous system
po — by mouth
prn — as needed
PS — prescription
PTA — prior to admission
PVC — premature ventricular
  contraction
Px — physical examination
Q — every
qd — every day
qh — every hour
qid — four times a day
qm — every morning
qn — every night
QNS — quantity not sufficient
qod — every other day
qs — enough
R — respiration
RBC — red blood count
REM — rapid eye movement
R/O — rule out
ROM — range of motion
ROS — review of systems

RR — recovery room
RTC — return to clinic
RTW — return to work
Rx — prescription, treatment
s̄ — without
S — subjective
SB — stillbirth
SCC — squamous cell carcinoma
S&O — salpingo-oophorectomy
SOB — shortness of breath
SPP — suprapubic prostatectomy
SP — spinal
S/P — status post
SUBQ — subcutaneous
SRG — surgery
SX — symptoms
Sx — signs
T — temperature
T&A — tonsillectomy and
    adenoidectomy
TAB — therapeutic abortion
TAH — total abdominal hysterec
tomy
TBLC — term birth, living child
TC — throat culture
TIA — transient ischemic attack
tid — three times a day

TL — tubal ligation
TPR — temperature, pulse,
    respiration
TURP — transurethral resection of
    prostate
TVH — total vaginal hysterectomy
IA — urinalysis
U&C — usual and customary
UCHD — usual childhood diseases
UK — unknown
URI — upper respiratory infection
UTI — urinary tract infection
V — vein
VDRL — venereal disease
    research laboratory (syphilis)
VS — vital signs
VSS — vital signs stable
W — widowed
WBC — white blood cells
WDWN — well-developed,
    well-nourished
WF — white female
WM — white male
WNL — within normal limits
XM — crossmatch
YO — year old
? — question of

APPENDIX C: PROFESSIONAL AND DISEASE-SPECIFIC ORGANIZATIONS

PROFESSIONAL ORGANIZATIONS

Academy of Psychosomatic
  Medicine
70 W. Hubbard St., Suite 202,
Chicago, IL 60610

American Academy of Health
  Administration
5530 Wisconsin Ave., NW
Suite 745,
Washington, DC 20815

American Association For The
  Study of Headache
5252 N. Western Ave.,
Chicago, IL 60625

American Burn Association
1130 E. McDowell, B-2,
Phoenix, AZ 85006

American Pain Society
70 W. Hubbard, Suite 202,
Chicago, IL 60610

American Psychological
  Association
1200 17th St., NW
Washington, DC 20036

American Psychosomatic Society
265 Nassau Rd.
Roosevelt, NY 11575

American Society of Clinical
  Hypnosis
2250 E. Devon Ave., Suite 336,
Des Plaines, IL 60018

American Society of Clinical
  Oncology
435 N. Michigan Ave., Suite 1717,
Chicago, IL 60611

Association for Health Care
  Quality
3550 Woodlan Rd.,
Ann Arbor, NI 48104

Arthritis Health Professions
  Association
1314 Spring St., NW
Atlanta, GA 30309

Biofeedback Society of America
4301 Owens St.,
Wheat Ridge, CO 80033

Gerontological Society of America
1411 K St., NW, Suite 300,
Washington, DC 20005

Health Education Foundation
600 New Hampshire Ave., NW,
Suite 452,
Washington, DC 20037

International Association For The
   Study of Pain
909 N. E. 43rd St., Suite 204,
Seattle, WA 98105

National Migraine Foundation
5252 N. Western Ave.,
Chicago, IL 60625

Society of Behavioral Medicine
P.O. Box 8530,
University Station,
Knoxville, TN 37996

DISEASE-SPECIFIC ORGANIZATIONS

American Anorexia/Bulimia
   Association
133 Cedar Lane,
Teaneck,NJ 07666

American Behcet's Foundation
110 E. 16th St.,
Santa Ana, CA 92701

American Brittle Bone Society
1256 Merrill Drive,
West Chester, PA 19382

American Cancer Society
90 Park Avenue,
New York, NY 10016

American Diabetes Association
Two Park Avenue,
New York, NY 10016

American Digestive Disease
   Society
7720 Wisconsin Ave.,
Bethesda, MD 20814

American Heart Association
7320 Greenville Ave.,
Dallas, TX 75231

American Liver Foundation
998 Pompton Ave.,
Cedar Grove, NJ 07009

American Lung Association
3740 Broadway,
New York, NY 10019

American Paralysis Association
275 One Lincoln Centre,
5400 LBJ Freeway,
Dallas, TX 75240

American Tinnitus Association
P.O. Box 5,
Portland, OR 97207

Arthritis Foundation
1314 Spring St., NW
Atlanta, GA 30309

Association of Birth Defect
   Children
3526 Emerywood Ln.,
Orlando, FL 32806

Cystic Fibrosis Foundation
6000 Executive Blvd., Suite 309,
Rockville, MD 50852

Dystonia Medical Research
  Foundation
9615 Brighton Way, Suite 416,
Beverly Hills, CA 90210

Huntington's Disease Foundation
  of America
250 W. 57th St., Suite 2016,
New York, NY 10107

Lupus Foundation of America
11921A Olive Blvd.,
St. Louis, MO 63141

Muscular Dystrophy Association
810 Seventh Ave.,
New York, NY 10019

Myasthenia Gravis Foundation
15 E. 26th St., Suite 1603,
New York, NY 10010

National Association For Hearing
  and Speech Action
10801 Rockville Pike,
Rockville, MD 20852

National Head Injury Foundation
18A Vernon St.,
Framingham, MA 01701

National Hospice Organization
1901 N. Ft. Myer Dr., #402,
Arlington, VA 22209

National Kidney Foundation
Two Park Ave.,
New York, NY 10016

National Reye's Syndrome
  Foundation
426 N. Lewis,
Bryan, OH 43506

National Sudden Infant Death
  Syndrome Clearinghouse
3520 Prospect St., NW,
Ground Floor, Suite 1,
Washington, DC 20057

Paget's Disease Foundation
P.O. Box 2772,
Brooklyn, NY 11202

Parkinson's Educational Program
1800 Park Newport, #302,
Newport Beach, CA 92660

People with AIDS
Box G27, 444 Houston St.,
New York, NY 10011

Spina Bifida Association of
  America
343 S. Dearborn Ave., #317,
Chicago, IL 60604

United Parkinson Foundation
360 W. Superior St.,
Chicago, IL 60610

Author Index

Ader, R.   4
Adler, N. E.   5, 17
Agras, W. W.   96, 97, 99, 106
Alexander, F.   3
American Psychological Association   4, 12, 13, 19, 20, 26, 30, 31, 32, 49, 50, 51, 64
Andrasik, F.   109
Andrykowski, M. A.   109
Araujo, D. M.   119
Asken, M. J.   2, 11

Bagheri, A. S.   119
Bandura, A.   104
Barton, W. E.   42
Bazelon, D. L.   44
Beck, A. T.   84, 108
Beecher, H. K.   36
Beigler, J. S.   62
Belar, C. D.   10, 11, 12, 13, 87, 103
Bergner, M.   85
Berman, P. S.   86
Bernhard, R.   84
Bernstein, D. A.   101
Bersoff, D. N.   49, 51
Billowitz, A.   27
Binner, P. R.   30
Bird, P. O.   99
Blackwell, K.   26
Blanchard, E. B.   109
Blumenthal, J. A.   71, 81, 88
Bobbitt, R. A.   85
Borkovec, T. D.   101
Bradley, L. A.   5, 17, 48, 71, 88, 96, 109, 139
Broadman, K.   85
Brodsky, A.   43, 59, 60

Brucker, B. S.   110
Burish, T. G.   109
Burns, M.   103
Bursztajn, H.   43, 59, 60
Butcher, J. N.   49

Cacioppo. J. T.   86
Carrington, C.   12
Carter, W. B.   85
Cash, H.   84
Cassileth, B. R.   43
Catell, R. B.   84
Cautela, J. R.   101
Clayman, D. A.   7, 139
Cohen, F.   5, 17
Cohen, L. H.   33
Cohen, R. J.   42, 55, 57, 67, 68
Corah, N. L.   85
Cross, H. K.   45, 53, 54, 59, 68
Cummings, N. A.   138, 139

DaBell, R.   27
Davis, M.   99, 101
Davis, R.   106
Davison, G.   108
Dawidoff, D.   55
Deardorff, W. W.   45, 53, 54, 58, 59, 68
DeBoer, K. F.   101
DeGood, D. E.   122
Delgado, A.   84
DePiano, F. A.   102
Derogatis, L. R.   82, 84
Diller, L.   110
Downs, H.   84
Dubin, S. S.   35

Dunn, M. E.   106

Eber, H. W.   84
Eisenberg, L.   36
Elfant, A. B.   24
Ellis, A.   108
Emery, G.   108
Engel, G. L.   6, 10, 36, 71
Erdman, A. J.   85
Eschelman, E. R.   101

Fabrega, H.   36
Fanning, P.   99
Feldman, S. R.   53
Feuerstein, M.   17, 99
Fisher, K.   53
Fleck, S.   79
Follick, M. J.   10
Folstein, M. F.   84
Folstein, S. E.   84
Fordyce, W. E.   106
Fowler, R. D.   49
Frank, J. D.   96
Friedson, W.   27
Furrow, B.   53, 55, 68

Gable, R. K.   68
Genest, M.   101
Gentry, W. D.   2, 4, 5, 11, 17
Gertman, P. M.   85
Gil, K.   98, 109
Gilson, B. S.   85
Glover, S. I.   52, 55
Goldfried, M. R.   108
Good, B.   36
Goodstein, L. D.   63
Gordon, W. A.   110
Gorsuch, R. L.   84
Graham, J. R.   48
Green, C. J.   5, 17, 48, 84
Greenberg, S.   97
Greene, R. L.   48
Grimaldi, K. E.   106
Gross, B. H.   61, 62, 63
Grotz, R.   84
Gruen, W.   97
Grunder, T. M.   42

Hall, J. E.   33
Halperin, D. A.   42

Hamilton, M.   86
Hamm, R. M.   43, 59, 60
Harris, M.   53
Harwick, R. D.   29
Hathaway, S. A.   83
Hay, D.   110
Haynes, R. B.   109
Heide, F. J.   100
Herd, J. A.   110
Herrera, J.   103
Hofer, P. J.   49, 51
Hogan, D.   59
Holmes, T. H.   84
Holzman, A. D.   109
Hughes, H.   11
Hupprich, W.   53, 68

Jacobs, D. F.   32
Jacobs, J.   84
Jacobson, E.   99
Janis, I. L.   5
Jenkins, C. D.   85
Johnson, J. H.   84, 86
Jones, E.   127

Kamenar, P. D.   61, 62
Kao, D.   103
Karoly, P.   71, 81, 88
Katz, S. T.   84
Keefe, F. J.   71, 81, 88
Keith-Spiegel, P.   26, 51
Kendall, P. C.   98, 109
Kibrick, S.   103
Kimball, W. H.   102
Klein, J. I.   52, 55
Kleinman, A.   36, 37, 123
Kline, F. M.   119
Knapp, S.   42, 53, 54, 55, 56, 57, 62, 68
Koocher, G. P.   26, 39, 51
Korchin, S. J.   98
Kornfield, D. S.   109
Kuczmierczyk, A. R.   17, 99

Labbe, E. E.   17, 99
Lane, L. S.   119
Lang, P. J.   106
LeCron, L.   102
Leigh, H.   71
Leo, J.   127

Leventhal, H.   110
Levy, S.   109
Ley, P.   42, 105
Libet, J.   106
Lichtenstein, E.   106
Lipowski, Z. J.   3, 10, 25, 30, 69, 70
Loeser, J. K. D.   46
Lucente, F. E.   79
Lushene, R.   84
Luthe, ,,W.   100

Madison, R.   103
Magrab, P. R.   106
March, V.   43
Mariano, W. E.   42
Markus, R. M.   54
Marshall-Goodell, B.   86
Masek, B. J.   99
Maslach, C.   110
Mason, J. H.   85
Masur, F. T.   11, 109
Matarazzo, J.   1, 2, 10, 49, 50, 110
Matthews, K.   82
McHugh, P. R.   84
McKay, M.   99, 101, 108
McKinley, J. C.   83
Meagher, R. B.   5, 17, 84
Mechanic, D.   36
Meenan, R. F.   85
Meichenbaum, D.   101, 108
Melamed, B. G.   104, 106
Melzack, R.   36, 85
Mesibov, G. B.   8
Miller, N. E.   10, 32, 110
Millon, T.   1, 5, 10, 17, 84
Moos, B.   84
Moos, R. H.   84, 85, 88, 109
Morrow, G.   7
Murray, H. A.   84

Nader, R.   26
Nerenz, D. R.   110
Newman, A. S.   51, 67
Nisbett, R.   127
Noll, J. D.   44
Noonberg, A. R.   102, 103, 110

Oken, D.   110

Olton, D. S.   102, 103, 110
Osler, W.   69

Papadopoulu, Z. L.   106
Peterson, L.   27
Petkas, P.   26
Petrucci, R. J.   29
Petty, R. E.   86
Philips, C.   86
Pope, K. S.   54
Prokop, C. K.   5, 17, 48, 71, 88, 96, 139

Quinn, K. M.   62

Raczynski, J. M.   102
Rahe, R. H.   84
Ray, W. J.   102
Redd, W. H.   109
Reiser, M. F.   71
Rodin, J.   10
Rogers, T.   102
Rorer, L. G.   42
Rorschach, H.   84
Rosenbaum, L.   93
Rosenman, R.   82, 85
Rush, A. J.   108
Russo, D. C.   99

Sackett, D. L.   109
Sadoff, R. L.   63
Sajwaj, T.   106
Sales, B. D.   30, 51
Samuels, M.   101
Samuels, N.   101
Sanborn, C. J.   42
Sarason, I. G.   84
Schenkenberg, T.   27
Schindler, R. J.   62
Schofield, W.   5, 10
Schultz, J. H.   100
Schutz, B. M.   42, 53, 68
Schwartz, G. E.   2, 137
Schwitzgebel, R. K.   62
Schwitzgebel, R. L.   62
Seeburg, K. N.   101
Selzberg, H. C.   102
Shapiro, A. K.   96
Shaw, B. F.   108

Shevitz, S. A.   70, 128
Shows, W. D.   27
Siegel, J. M.   84
Siegel, L. J.   11, 12, 104
Silberfarb, P. M.   70
Singer, J. E.   10
Slovenko, R.   54
Smith, Jr., L. H.   15
Southard, M. J.   61, 62, 63
Spielberger, C. D.   84
Stabler, B.   8
Stone, A. A.   42
Stone, G. E.   5, 10, 12, 17, 18, 110
Strain, J. J.   84
Street, W. J.   11
Stricker, G.   30, 32, 33
Sutton, E.   86
Sutton-Smith, K.   43
Swencionis, C.   33

Tarshis, C. B.   55
Tavel, E. B.   12
Taylor, D. W.   109
Theamann, M.   33
Tiep, B. L.   103
Turk, D. C.   101, 108, 109
Turkington, C.   53

VandeCreek, L.   42, 53, 54, 55, 56, 57, 68

Wall, P. D.   36
Ward, T. M.   53
Warner, R. M.   79
Watson, D.   98, 109
Weiner, H.   5, 17
Weisenberg, M.   102
Weisman, A. D.   122
Weiss, S. M.   2, 10, 110, 136
Wettstein, R. M.   62
Widiger, T. A.   42
Williams, R. B.   5
Wilson, E.   11
Wolf, S.   3
Wolff, H. G.   3, 85
Wolpe, J.   104
Wood, D.   27
Worden, J. W.   109
Wright, R. H.   53, 65, 67
Wynguarden, J. B.   15

Zerubavel, E.   33, 34
Zupkis, R. V.   43
Zyzanski, S. J.   85

Subject Index

Accountability 32–33
Advertising and endorsements 39–40
American Psychosomatic Society 15
American Psychological Association
  Accreditation Handbook 13
  Ethical Principles of Psychologists 31, 50
  Hospital Primer for Psychologists, 19–20, 30
  internships 11
  Standards for Providers of Psychological Services 31, 51
Arden House National Working Conference 5, 12, 34
Archival data, in assessment 87
Arthritis Impact Measurement Scale 83
Assessment
  and the referral question 112–113
  communication of the results of 131–133
  diagnostic issues related to 69–70
  integrating the basic information of 78–81, 87–88
  methods of 81–87
  neglecting the context of 127
  problems in gathering information of 116–118
  targets of 72–78
Assessment targets
  affective 73–74
  behavioral 73, 75
  biological 72–74
  cognitive 73, 75
  environmental 76–78

Beck Depression Inventory 84
Behavioral Medicine 2
Behavioural rehearsal 105–106

Biofeedback 86, 102–104, 110
Biofeedback Society of America 15
Burnout 110

Charting
  and problems in confidentiality 64
  and problems with poor handwriting 118
  techniques 131–133
Clinical health psychology (*see also* Professional practice)
  core content of 13–14
  current role and functions of practitioners in 7–10
  defining the field of 1–3
  education in 11–17
  expansion of the field of 4–5
  future issues in 135
  growth of knowledge in 137–138
  historical perspectives in 3–4
  reference materials in 15
  supervised training in 16–17
Cognitive Capacity Screening Exam 84
Cognitive intervention strategies 107–108
Compliance with treatment 109
Computerized psychological testing 49–50
Confidentiality
  breach of 61, 64
  ethical principle of 40
  problems in obtaining release of 117
  release of 65
  special problems of, in clinical health psychology 40–41, 64–65
  versus privileged information 40
Contingency management 106–107

Coping with chronic illness   109
Cornell Medical Index   85
Crisis intervention   98
Cuing   107
Cultural issues in practice   36–37

Death and dying   109
Dental Anxiety Scale   85
Diagnosis (*see also* Psychological
    evaluation)
    medical versus psychological   55–56
Diaries, in assessment   83
Disposition, in treatment   130–131
Division of Health Psychology   8, 15
DRGs   21
Dumping   116

Education in health psychology (*see also*
    Clinical health psychology)   11–17
Ethical principles
    assessment techniques   47–50
    competence   34–37
    confidentiality   40–41
    moral and legal standards   37–38
    professional relationships   46–47
    public statements   38–40
    responsibility   31–34
    welfare of the consumer   41–46

Family Environment Scale   84

Goals, in treatment   94

Health care
    changes in the system of   138
    education in   14
    psychology's role in   5–7
    responsibility for the quality of   32–34
Health care settings
    effects on patient assessment   79–80
    effects on treatment   109–110
    formalized aspects of   19–21
    informal aspects of   22–23
Health psychology
    core content areas of   13–14, 17
    definition of   1, 10
    training programs in   11–13

Hospital Primer for Psychologists   19
Hospital staff privileges   19–21
Hypnosis   102
Hypothesis testing   119–120, 128

Illness prevention   110
Imagery   101–102
Index of Activities of Daily Living   84
Informed consent
    elements of   42
    in psychological evaluation   48
    problems in   42–44
Intervention strategies   95–108
    and cooperation of the staff   94–95,
        115–116
    and the hostile patient   121–125
    and the referral question   113–114
    choosing the appropriate provider in
        114
    initial contact with the patient and
        119–120
Intervention targets
    and goal setting   94
    environmental   90–92
    interrelationship among   93–94
    patient   89–90
    sociocultural   92
Interview, clinical   81–82, 119, 121–125

Jenkins Activity Survey   85
Joint Commission on Accreditation of
        Hospitals   21, 131
Journals in clinical health psychology
        149–150

Life events, measures of   84

Malpractice in clinical health psychology
    areas of risk   55–68
    definition of   53–55, 68
    minimizing the risk of   66–67
McGill Pain Questionnaire   85
Medical abbreviations   15, 151–154
Medical expertise, lack of   117
Medical psychology   2
Medicine
    interacting with the field of   23–26
    overidentification with   24

professional relationships with   46
stereotypes in   27
Millon Behavioral Health Inventory   84
Mind–body dualism
  in administrative structures   7
  in health policies   5
  in practice   5–6, 28
Mini-Mental State Exam   84
MMPI   47, 83–84
Modeling   104–105

Nudity of the patient, dealing with   126

Observation, in assessment   85–86

Patient advocacy   25, 44
Patient attitudes, dealing with hostile
    patient   121–125
Pain management   109
Patient education   42–43, 97–98, 123
Peer review   30, 32–33
Personal problems in practice   27–30,
    37–38
Physician, communicating with   131–132
Placebo effect   96
Professional Organizations   155–157
Professional practice
  and cross referrals   137
  areas of clinical service   70–71
  boundary issues in   125–126
  ethical principles of   31–51
  personal characteristics in   26–30
  preparation for   18–30
  settings of   18
Projective techniques   84
Psychiatry, changes in   138
Psychological evaluation
  assessment instruments of   83–85
  ethical aspects of   47–50
  informed consent for   44
  of medical patients   47–48
  malpractice risks in   65–67
  third party requests for   44–45
Psychometric assessment   83–85, 126–127
Psychopathology   127–128
Psychophysiological assessment   86
Psychosomatic medicine   2, 10
Psychotherapy   96–97

Quality assurance   32–33
Questionnaires, in assessment   82–83

Referral
  customs   22–23
  determining the reasons for   111–112,
    128
  timing of   115–116
Rehabilitation medicine   110
Relaxation training   99–101
Report writing   24, 131–132

Scheduling of patients   119–121
Self-monitoring   107
Sickness Impact Profile   85
Side effects of medical treatment   109
Skills training   105–106
Society of Behavioral Medicine   15
Specialization in clinical health psychology
    136–137
State–Trait Anxiety Inventory   84
Stressful medical procedures, preparation
    for   109
Suicide
  precautions in management   61
  preventing patients from harming
    themselves   58–61
  treatment decisions related to   59–61
Supervision in clinical health psychology
    16–17, 51, 67–68
Symptom Checklist   90, 94
Systematic desensitization   104

Tarasoff decision   61–64
The 16 Personality Factor Inventory   84
Therapeutic contract   129–130
Touching by the therapist   126
Treatment (see also Intervention strategies)
  determining an adequate trial of   129
  follow-up in   24, 131–134
  interruption of   130
  patients who do not benefit from   45
  when to refer for   133
Turfing   116

Ward Atmosphere Scale   85
Work Environment Scale   85

ABOUT THE AUTHORS

Cynthia D. Belar received her PhD from Ohio University in 1974, after an internship at Duke University Medical Center. From 1974 to 1984 she was on the faculty of the Department of Clinical Psychology at the University of Florida's academic medical center. Since 1984 she has served as Chief Psychologist and Clinical Director of Behavioral Medicine for the Kaiser Permanente Medical Care Program in Los Angeles. She has also served as Chair, Education and Training Committee, Division of Health Psychology; Chair, Graduate Education and Training Committee of the American Psychological Association; and Chair, Executive Committee, Association of Psychology Internship Centers.

William W. Deardorff received his doctorate in clinical psychology from Washington State University in 1985, after an internship at University of Washington Medical School. He then completed a postdoctoral fellowship in clinical health psychology in the Kaiser Permanente Medical Care Program, Los Angeles. He is currently in private practice, specializing in clinical health psychology at the Treatment Center for Craniomandibular Disorders in Woodland Hills, California. His research and clinical interests include pain, psychological factors in medical disorders, and legal and ethical issues in psychotherapy.

Karen E. Kelly received her doctorate in clinical psychology from the University of Kansas in 1985. After an internship at Veterans Administration Medical Center, Long Beach, she completed a postdoctoral fellowship in clinical health psychology at Kaiser Permanente Medical Center, Los Angeles. She is currently a staff psychologist in the Department of Physical Medicine and Rehabilitation at Cedars Sinai Medical Center, Los Angeles. Her research interests include Type A behavior in women, psychosocial interactions with medical disorders, and the efficacy of pain management programs.

Psychology Practitioner Guidebooks

Editors
Arnold P. Goldstein, Syracuse University
Leonard Krasner, Stanford University & SUNY at Stony Brook
Sol L. Garfield, Washington University

Elsie M. Pinkston & Nathan L. Linsk — CARE OF THE ELDERLY:
A Family Approach
Donald Meichenbaum — STRESS INOCULATION TRAINING
Sebastiano Santostefano — COGNITIVE CONTROL THERAPY
WITH CHILDREN AND ADOLESCENTS
Lillie Weiss, Melanie Katzman & Sharlene Wolchik — TREATING
BULIMIA: A Psychoeducational Approach
Edward B. Blanchard & Frank Andrasik — MANAGEMENT OF
CHRONIC HEADACHES: A Psychological Approach
Raymond G. Romanczyk — CLINICAL UTILIZATION OF
MICROCOMPUTER TECHNOLOGY
Philip H. Bornstein & Marcy T. Bornstein — MARITAL THERAPY:
A Behavioral-Communications Approach
Michael T. Nietzel & Ronald C. Dillehay — PSYCHOLOGICAL
CONSULTATION IN THE COURTROOM
Elizabeth B. Yost, Larry E. Beutler, M. Anne Corbishley & James R.
Allender — GROUP COGNITIVE THERAPY: A Treatment
Method for Depressed Older Adults
Lillie Weiss — DREAM ANALYSIS IN PSYCHOTHERAPY
Edward A. Kirby & Liam K. Grimley — UNDERSTANDING AND
TREATING ATTENTION DEFICIT DISORDER
Jon Eisenson — LANGUAGE AND SPEECH DISORDERS
IN CHILDREN
Eva L. Feindler & Randolph B. Ecton — ADOLESCENT ANGER
CONTROL: Cognitive-Behavioral Techniques
Michael C. Roberts — PEDIATRIC PSYCHOLOGY: Psychological
Interventions and Strategies for Pediatric Problems
Daniel S. Kirschenbaum, William G. Johnson & Peter M. Stalonas, Jr. —
TREATING CHILDHOOD AND ADOLESCENT OBESITY
W. Stewart Agras — EATING DISORDERS: Management of Obesity,
Bulimia and Anorexia Nervosa
Ian H. Gotlib & Catherine A. Colby — TREATMENT OF DEPRESSION:
An Interpersonal Systems Approach
Walter B. Pryzwansky & Robert N. Wendt — PSYCHOLOGY AS A
PROFESSION: Foundations of Practice
Cynthia D. Belar, William W. Deardorff & Karen E. Kelly — THE
PRACTICE OF CLINICAL HEALTH PSYCHOLOGY
Paul Karoly & Mark P. Jensen — MULTIMETHOD ASSESSMENT
OF CHRONIC PAIN

Pergamon Titles of Related Interest

Agras EATING DISORDERS:
Management of Obesity, Bulimia and Anorexia Nervosa

Blanchard/Andrasik MANAGEMENT OF CHRONIC
HEADACHES:
A Psychological Approach

Blechman/Brownell HANDBOOK OF BEHAVIORAL MEDICINE
FOR WOMEN

DiMatteo/DiNicola ACHIEVING PATIENT COMPLIANCE:
The Psychology of the Medical Practitioner's Role

Holzman/Turk MANAGEMENT OF CHRONIC PAIN:
A Handbook of Psychological Treatment Approaches

Karoly/Steffen/O'Grady CHILD HEALTH PSYCHOLOGY:
Concepts and Issues

Meichenbaum STRESS INOCULATION TRAINING

Russell STRESS MANAGEMENT FOR CHRONIC DISEASE

Van Hasselt/Strain/Hersen HANDBOOK OF DEVELOPMENTAL
AND PHYSICAL DISABILITIES

Varni CLINICAL BEHAVIORAL PEDIATRICS:
An Interdisciplinary Biobehavioral Approach

Weiss/Katzman/Wolchik TREATING BULIMIA:
A Psychoeducational Approach

Related Journals
(Free sample copies available upon request)

CLINICAL PSYCHOLOGY REVIEW
SOCIAL SCIENCE & MEDICINE
ARCHIVES OF CLINICAL NEUROPSYCHOLOGY

William L. Golden, E. Thomas Dowd & Fred Friedberg —
   HYPNOTHERAPY: A Modern Approach
Patricia Lacks — BEHAVIORAL TREATMENT FOR PERSISTENT
   INSOMNIA
Arnold P. Goldstein & Harold Keller — AGGRESSIVE BEHAVIOR:
   Assessment and Intervention
C. Eugene Walker, Barbara L. Bonner & Keith L. Kaufman — THE
   PHYSICALLY AND SEXUALLY ABUSED CHILD: Evaluation and
   Treatment
Robert E. Becker, Richard G. Heimberg & Alan S. Bellack — SOCIAL
   SKILLS TRAINING TREATMENT FOR DEPRESSION